Connections

Connections

letter poems to family and friends around the world

Richard M. Grove

Aeolus House

Editors – Dr. Jaydeep Sarangi and Allan Briesmaster
Cover Photograph – Richard M. Grove
Cover Design and Typography – Richard M. Grove

Library and Archives Canada Cataloguing in Publication

Title: Connections : letter poems to family and friends around the world / Richard M. Grove.
Names: Grove, Richard M. (Richard Marvin), author
Identifiers: Canadiana 20250259583 | ISBN 9781987872750 (softcover)
Subjects: LCGFT: Poetry.
Classification: LCC PS8563.R75 C66 2025 | DDC C811/.54—dc23

Published by
Aeolus House
P.O. Box 53031
Royal Orchard Postal Station
10 Royal Orchard Blvd.
Thornhill, ON L3T 3C0
www.aeolushouse.com

Printed and bound in Canada
Distributed in USA by Ingram

This collection is dedicated to
Kim,
my darling late wife
and life partner of 31 years.

At Our Beach

for Kim

Thursday April 17, 2008

My Dear Kimber,

You are in Chicago,
maybe just landed,
making your way to luggage,
taxi, then hotel.
You will strip
your virgin bar of soap
of its pretentious wrapper
that says new.
You will dine with colleagues,
orange juice and maybe luscious
crepes you like so much.
I am not ... remotely jealous
that you are there in the breezy city,
for I am here on our Lake Ontario beach.
The honking that I hear
is Canada Geese as they V
their way to their summer home
over Buffelheads diving, feeding.
I am at last year's picnic table soaking
up tranquility's lapping shore
in mellow embrace
thinking of you.

I love you and miss you,
Tai
xxoo

sparks from Love's kisses
for Kim

June 2015

My Darling,

Remember the fireflies
we saw on that June night.
Holding hands we were walking
in the dark, home, down the hill
toward the silent silver lake.
A slight cool breeze in the stillness
rustled leaves,
stirring grass to sway.

Remember the thousands of fireflies
blinking in the almost pitch black,
so dark, shoulder to shoulder
we could hardly see our feet.
Silhouettes of trees floated
against a midnight sky.
The air was full, the aroma of spring
wafted gently over your shoulder,
you becoming the blossomed trees.
A distant train wailed
its muffled mourning
in the veil of iridescent mist
that made you glow.

Remember the fireflies.
They were sparks from Love's kisses.
Flickers of divine inspiration,
emanating from the ethereal.

Remember the fireflies.
They were my silent unspoken
love for you
in the stillness of our walk.

Love,
Tai
xxoo

Contents

To Basu in India

Covid Poems

Letters Home from Cuba

Introduction

Tai's letter poems are very much friendship poems; friendships for whom Tai cares deeply. Written with a great degree of sincerity and honesty these poems often break boundaries of nations. With a soulful tone Tai often weaves the stories of relationships, human predicaments and lost moments. He transforms them with vital energy like the committed artist he is. For him, it is difficult to leave the space, once it is fixed to his name, links and roles. The poet explores how everything is, lives and breathes or simply just ceases to be. Every special intimacy is a smile in a moment of time. The poet walks along the sandy shores of the river of life and realises that lost moments are not lost forever. These moments often ride on horsebacks and invade the kingdom of the past, present and future. For Tai, lost keys search for their former locks.

This deeply meditative poet looks at the flight of the sparrows of life. Their twitter unfolds memories of the world. Through these often simple but well-crafted letter poems the poet seems to realise that there is no definite destination for him. His walk has no destination, yet he must walk.

Poems in this confident collection deeply meditate upon human relationships, the places, the seasons of memory, the human solitariness, the simple daily happenings, even the crispness of the air. The unpretentious clarity these poems bring reflect the poet's subtle mind. Tai is a committed soul maker. With these letter poems he takes us on a journey where the world is mapped through the doors of hearts.

In some poems the past leans silently. The sensuous poet captures an atmosphere of a wintry evening where mist and chill deepens after the sun sets. In a mood of retrospection the poet remembers a loving soul from a distant land or a missed family member. What can separation of hearts lead to? Love acts rise and fall. Poor human beings have no control of hearts of others. Tai makes darkness palpable and light tangible. Life's fairy story sees good and light in the deepest darkness. Tai sometimes writes to people whom he has never met but he captures emotions attached to these relationships/friendships between two distant poetic minds living on different continents. With these letter poems Tai is a champion map maker reaching across oceans.

"Dear Basu" is written to a fellow poet halfway around the world with whom he has never met,

> *Dear Basu,*
>
> *even though*
> *in a haste to go to bed —*
> *midnight barking at my heels —*
> *i managed to tap out*
> *a quick review of your book —*
> *see attached.*
> *i hope it is worthy*
> *of your fine work.*

Many of his poems are descriptive. He portrays things vividly with lucidly, as in this excerpt,

> *Morning is gently rising at 1050 km/hr*
> *from a painful,*
> *sleepless, almost seven hour flight.*
> *12:40am Toronto time*
> *5:40am sun-time*
> *We fly over jolly old England.*
> *Glaswegians' morning alarms are now raising*
> *the workers of life as we jet overhead*
> *past Newcastle, on into Amsterdam.*

Tai's poem(s) for Miguel is mesmerizing and soul touching. Cuba and Canada occupy special space in the mind of the poet:

> *It's a hot one today.*
> *The same in Cuba I presume.*
> *Here it was 23°C at 9am. Climbed*
> *to a promised brow-dripping 34°C.*
> *A fire-breathing dragon chased me*
> *to the lumberyard*
> *to buy some wood for a shelf*
> *that was on my honey-dew list,*

Writing to his dear friend John B. Lee, Tai makes reference to Manuel, Miguel and Jorge. All four are not only poets but also soul makers for this poet. Tai is a poet of friendships on many different levels. He is a silent watcher on the fringes of life, as seen in this excerpt,

> *Kim and I are just back*
> *from a trip up to our friends'*
> *privately-owned land.*
> *I said to Kim*
> *one day when we were at the top*
> *of their very own small mountain,*
> *their vista sharing boundaries with*
> *Algonquin Provincial Park,*
> *that I wish we could share*
> *this awe-inspiring panorama*
> *with our dear Cuban friends,*
> *Manuel, Jorge and Miguel.*

Further expressions of brotherly love can be found in this covid excerpt,

> *Friends in Gibara Cuba,*
> *brother and sister Jorge and Michelle*
> *say that family are mostly mask free now.*
> *Dinner with their priest*
> *will bring in the new year*
> *with a covid prayer of safety for all.*
> *By the way I heard he has covid now.*
> *Their friends are gathering*
> *for a roasted pig,*
> *Let's hope everyone stays outdoors*
> *and stays safe.*

The veteran poet beautifully creates a vivid stillness of people waiting for mellow fruitfulness in their lives. Silence is pronounced as the most important aspect of these beguilingly simple poems. Tai's thoughts are hopeful at the core, redolent with mysterious colours of the imagination. Mundane wishes come and go. As a thoughtful poet, through and through, he has a sensitive heart to feel all these arrivals and departures of wishes and dreams.

Read during different shades of the mind, Tai's poetry outbreaks daylight. For him, writing poetry is a night clearing act which takes the reader beyond the 'stories of the night.' – The night carries itself far into the day. These letter poems are actually memories in words, dreams of returning, life's longing and hope, where leaf by leaf this magician knocks at the multiple doors of hearts. These poems show how humans have more resilience than flowers, more elasticity than insects and birds.

With this beautifully crafted collection of letter poems Tai makes the contemporary world of poetry stronger!

The Editor,
Dr. Jaydeep Sarangi
Poet, Editor, Professor,
State Level Mentor for NAAC
President, Guild of Indian English Writers
Principal at New Alipore College, Kolkata, India
Vice President, EC, Intercultural Poetry and Performance Library

Preface

As I was pulling together my letter poems for Jaydeep I was wondering when and how I started writing letters in the form of poems. First I reckoned that it was probably the result of the quick form of writing emails and the habit of writing short lines. This might partly be true but the fact is it has been my inclination to write short line letters for a long time. Maybe these short lines turned me into a poet.

I have turned, over time, into being what others describe as a descriptive writer who naturally describes the world around me the way I do as a photographer and as a painter. In my short stories and novels I am not heavy with the ins and outs of a thick plot. My prose, as with my poetry, relies more on description of scene and situation. The sky does not just turn into a beautiful sunset. It turns into the vibration of colour that shines through greying branches that rake the sky into dimming light.

So to my shock I found well over 100 letter poems that spanned not only across Canada but into Cuba, Bangladesh and India. I have loosely organized these letter poems into categories but did not so much worry about chronology of dates. In the end I left the order of the poems in the editorial hands of Jaydeep. As you will see, the first section of poems, after my dedication to my dear late wife Kim, are to Basu. As a fellow poet and editor in India she appreciated the poetics in my prose emails. A few of my shorter emails to her became letter poems.

Thank you Jaydeep for your interest in my letter poems and seeing the literary merit in this as a collection.

I would be remiss if at this stage I did not thank Allan Briesmaster; friend, fellow poet and fellow publisher for also seeing the literary value in this collection and offering to publish this book. I was chatting with Allan at a poetry reading some time ago bemoaning the fact that the publisher for this collection, in India, after sitting on the manuscript for well over a year, went out of business. Allan stepped up with no hesitation, offered to publish. With this task of publishing he also offered to edit, a bit of a smaller task after Jaydeep's editing and then on top of that his role as copy editor was much appreciated and valued considering my often copy edit blindness. I wince to think that I might have added any mistakes after his thorough input. Thank you Allan for your literary contribution to the success of this book and for all of your CanLit contributions over the years.

Richard M. Grove

Connections in Letter Poems and Photographs

I have been a photographer for many more years than I have been a poet. Over the years, I have had many exhibitions of my photography, including a solo show in Cuba. My most recent exhibition was at the Parrott Gallery in Belleville in November 2024. I began taking photographs seriously at the age of 13, after my father paid for half of my first single-lens reflex camera. This was an act of encouragement that deeply shaped not only my creativity but my general course in life.

Photography and poetry share a deep kinship for me. Both are creative acts that capture a specific moment in time, a fleeting instant when light, emotion, and meaning come together. For me, both are ways of saying: I see, I hear, and I am here with you. In this collection, poetry is the primary focus – pardon the pun. The photographs are woven together by the same impulse: to notice, to connect, and to bear witness to the quiet beauty that exists in everyday life.

The poems speak of love that crosses oceans, friendships sustained across continents, and everyday encounters that become moments of grace. Whether it is a grandson sending an "air hug" during the long isolation of a pandemic or a quiet morning walk shared with a squirrel, each poem finds meaning in relationships – personal, familial, or spiritual. They are letters of the heart, written to embrace, to hold, and to celebrate connection in all its forms.

The photographs echo the same sentiment found in the poems. They capture people as they truly are in private connections – talking in doorways, laughing by the sea, pausing in thought, cooking a meal together, giving a manicure, sharing a hug. These are not grand or staged moments; they are fragments of life, tender and real, where human connection is visible in gestures and faces. Like the poems, the images find beauty in the everyday: neighbours chatting, families gathering, travellers exchanging stories, children playing, or a simple touch between friends that speaks volumes.

This is not meant to be an ekphrastic book, where images inspire poems or vice versa. Together, the poems and photographs simply form a dialogue about connection. Both are about presence: being present for someone else, for a shared moment, for a fleeting but meaningful connection. In a world that often moves too fast and speaks too loudly, these works – poems and photographs – invite us to slow down, to look, to listen, and to remember that connection is everywhere, waiting to be experienced, if only we pause long enough to see it.

Richard M. Grove

Madawaska Poems

Weston Island Paradise

For Manuel, Jorge and Miguel

September 1, 2020

Dear John and Cathy,

Kim and I are just back
from a trip up to our friends'
privately-owned land.
I said to Kim
one day when we were at the top
of their very own small mountain,
their vista sharing boundaries with
Algonquin Provincial Park,
that I wish we could share
this awe-inspiring panorama
with our dear Cuban friends,
Manuel, Jorge and Miguel.

Our Cuban friends would
melt into disbelief at the vastness,
the enormity, the sheer incalculability
of our Canadian wilderness, our
staggering sprawl.

They have the glory of palm trees,
ocean, sun and sand —
all of which we are drawn to year after year —
but we have something else
that is amazing in its ancient unspoiled purity.

Standing at the top of Weston Island
in the middle of Victoria Lake,
we — meaning all of Canada — have
an ancient wilderness almost
untouched, very much unspoiled.

It is beyond breathtaking,
almost beyond comprehension
that such a vastness could exist.
I wish we could share this bonding experience
with you four amigos,
our mutually loved Cuban friends.

All the best,
Tai

Swimming Through Mist to Morning

for Laurence Hutchman after his Swimming to the Sun

Dear Laurence,

I crept from bed to early morning
mist-draped view. A lake-lapping
white-tailed deer joined me
in this majesty of stillness. Others
slept while I stood in silence
listening
to the hush-filled whisper of trees
bowing to holy quietude
under the silver glow of a new day.

I was joyfully chilly standing
on this dew-dampened dock,
towel draped over shoulders
contemplating
slipping into ebony abyss. The hush
that echoed before me,
from yawning Algonquin hills,
across mirrored mist to Weston Island,
filled dawn with a palpable peace.

With the silent slither of an otter
I slipped into rippled moon.

Thanks for your wonderful book
Swimming into the Sun

Tai
P.S. – Hi to Eva

a madawaska calm

after e. e. cummings

September 22, 2006

dear jorge,

an immemorial horizon
of setting sun
silence
distills into Victoria Lake
spilled with stars

thinking of you,
tai

A High Price To Pay

September 2

Dear Mom and Dad,

We did have a few sunny spots in the morning
after a rain-drenched night of thunder.
Hope dappled across hushed Victoria Lake
to our amber, sandy cove. Calm,
no lapping waves,
disturbed the ancient stillness
that lay from fog-cloaked chilly shore to shore.

I was determined to have an early morning swim.
In up to my ankles but tiptoed out,
in up to my knees but dashed out,
in up to my waist vigorously splashing
chilled morning onto chest, my face,
my shoulders before my gasping plunge.
It was cooler than nippy but worth the aching ears.
In the end it was worth the price to pay
for breakfast bragging rights
that I was the only one
to take the plunge that rather cool
end-of-summer morning.

And then there was stoic Peter
before bed that night. He calmly,
with no sense of rush, sun almost set,
strolled bare-chested, one calm intrepid step
after another into his mist-blanketed chilling dip.
Sun-setting ripples shimmered
from his calm gentle strokes.

The next day
as I was putting on my long-legged sweatpants
Kim was donning her swimsuit,
slipping quietly into fog wrapped stillness,
disappearing into the black depths of oblivion
only to pop up like a mysterious maid of the mist
unruffled by chilled depths.
Distant loons yodeled across breaking mist,
calling her the Deep-Water Dipper.

We will show you pictures sometime soon.

Hugs,
your #1 son,
Richard

A Morning of Solitude

September 9

Dear Mom and Dad,

Two lone cormorants sit, wings splayed
to warming morning sun, basking
on gently bobbing raft
pushed east by cool
late August placid breeze.
I sit in my red Adirondack chair,
facing Weston Island
past rippled, steel-grey Victoria Lake,
jacket zipped to neck,
legs outstretched to meager sun,
warming.
A post breakfast yawn closes my eyes
to six dallying Canada Geese
silently paddling
single file to nowhere.

All the best,
Richard

Duck Under the Bowing Branches

August 10

Dear Mom and Dad,

Paddle upwind, the pushing
against mother nature can be wonderful,
exhilarating, when you stop the push
and the drive, let your kayak rest.
It will gently, slowly turn and flow
effortlessly with the current.
You need not even steer but be sure to duck
every so often under the bowing branches,
brace yourself
for the occasional bump and grind
against red-flecked granite boulders,
time's poltergeist hiding
just under the water. Spin and even glide
backwards, you will find it so much fun
but be sure to get out
at the sand-soft shore's edge
before the rush
takes you over the waterfall.

Your gliding #1 son,
Richard

It Was a Grey Morning

September 4

Dear Mom and Dad,

Rain drizzled from low-hung branches.
Motionless.
It might sound like a cliché
but here at Madawaska Lodge
time actually does stand still
between one moment of harmony,
a soul-stirring stillness and a calm beauty
that begs one to contemplate
the meaning of life
beyond Victoria Lake's
distant fog-draped hills.

Hugs from the north,
Richard

The Commonality of Being

September 2

Dear Mom and Dad,

Canada Geese stand sentry,
marching back and forth
on new stone wall built
with ancient
buffeted Canadian shield boulders,
nibbling grass edge
as if executing their millennial
inherited grooming duty.
Hummingbirds dart
over veranda red chairs
to and from feeder as if
there was a purpose
to zipping
out of sight and back again.
There is no duty or purpose
to my reclined posture
other than to be at one
with the chatting,
darting red squirrel,
to be in union
with the tapping woodpecker
that dances up and down,
around the fog-dampened
trunk of time.

Hugs from Kim and me,
Richard

To Mom and Dad

Living in the Past

December 3, 2014

Dear Mom and Dad,

Kim and I are in a fancy
air-conditioned bus driving through
the breadbasket of Cuba,
the agricultural area in the middle of the island,
on our way to Universidad Ciego de Avila.
From time to time we drive past
a small windmill whirling in the morning breeze.
I think you know the kind I mean.
The kind we had at the back of our house
when we lived on the farm in Puslinch. I remember
seeing it from the bathroom window
when I was just a boy.
As we pass by
they are all graciously spinning in the sunrise,
gentle wind pumping water for the farms they service.
I was trying to remember if the windmill that we had
actually worked or not, or was it just a relic of the past,
a museum piece, long ago replaced
by the electric pump. Somehow I don't ever remember
seeing it in motion.

Your number-one-son,
Ricardo

The Definition of an Optimist

December 3, 2014

Dear Mom and Dad,

Here we are with our feet up in Cuba.
Yesterday Kim and I were introduced
to our dormitory room
at Universidad Ciego de Avila. The room was
optimistically cool.
The air conditioner purred quietly
to the long-blinking fluorescent bulb
that revealed our three-bed room.
We were greeted by a modern TV
of more than adequate size and a refrigerator
of similar dimensions.
The definition of an optimist is Kim seeing the TV
and totally expecting it to work.
The definition of a super optimist is Kim
thinking that if you wait a while longer
it will warm up and flicker to life.
The definition of an uber-super optimist
is, after the TV has finally turned on and Kim
adjusts the rabbit ears expecting to tune in a channel,
any channel. The definition of a happy optimist
is Kim watching a clear, in focus, Cuban documentary
in Spanish.

The definition of a realist
is Kim not expecting water to ever arrive
at the air-hissing pipe that dribbles
into the bathroom sink.

Your number-one-son,
Ricardo

Dinner with the Ciego de Avila Fishermen

December 6, 2014

Dear Mom and Dad,

One evening, Kim and I strolled
from our Cuban hotel looking for dinner.
Our destination was the restaurant
that stood on metal pylons,
a fifty-yard, bridge-swinging
distance from the lily-pad shore.
We were ushered to our far corner table
that looked over the cedar decking
where moonlight shattered
in the crow-blue, breeze-brushed lake.

Attached to the nautical-wired railing,
inches from our feet, was a white
fiberglass rowboat where two Cuban Mulattos
sat bobbing the evening away. Fishing line
wrapped around their nimble fingers
as they waited for the twitch of a fish's nibble.
A predicted jolt from an invisible fish,
matched by a quick jerk of the line snagged
a shimmering twelve-inch, whiskered catfish.
Hit on the head with an empty wine bottle
it was tossed to the belly of the boat.
A celebration with a tip of rum is short.
Hook is tossed back to ebony depths
for luck's temptation.

Kim and I enjoy their congeniality as we share
a few friendly words in Spanish
before they paddle to the star-lit shore.
We enjoy the irony of sharing our fish dinner
with two Cuban fishermen.

See you when we get home to Ontario,
Love, Kim and Richard

London to Berlin 2005

(a prelude poem before reading at the J. F. Kennedy Institute in Berlin)

Dear Mom and Dad,

We arrived in Berlin on Sunday
after two rather unpoetic
whirlwind days
of touring London.

Not a single poetic thought
fluttered in mind
as we dashed
    click click a few pictures
from the Tower of London
    click click
to the National Library
    click click a few more pictures
from the National Gallery
    click click
to London Bridge
    click click even more pics
from Big Ben
    click click
to Buckingham Palace
    click clickclickclick
    click click even more pictures.
Nothing poetic stirred
    click click
as I longed for two minutes
of mindful clarity.
I longed for a single millisecond
that would not be interrupted
with the clatter of a train's
screeching wheels
or the repetitious echo of
    "Mind the gap please"
as we got on and off

our many trains
from polished steel and glass
to foot-trodden, gum-stained concrete.

I longed to hear
the cheerful chirping
of a single bird,
I longed to feel
a silver breeze
stroke spring green.

Instead
the highlight of London
for me was
uploading those 400
digital snapshots
onto my laptop

in the hustle bustle of Starbucks.
A de-café café laté
became my only moment of calm.
The warm soothing froth,
cinnamon-sprinkled,
wiped away the torturous
steel stair memories
of "The Tube."
It cleared away the miles
of wobbly cobblestones
and the constant need
to look "The Wrong Way"
before crossing the street.

Let me tell you
what a pleasure it is
to be here in Berlin

where the birds do sing
and the sun does shine.

With the ghost of JFK
looming in your welcoming halls,
*Ich bin auch ein Berliner.**
I am also a Berliner.
Thank you
for having me here today.

Love,
Richard

* *Ich bin ein Berliner* is the famous sentence that
USA President John F. Kennedy used in a speech
in Berlin in June, 1963.

My Little Flake
of The Berlin Wall

Dear Mom and Dad,

I plucked a flake of old paint
with my fingertips
from the Berlin wall.
Painlessly pinching a symbol of history
that says I was there,
in the shadow of time,
even if ten years late.
I was witness,
even if only as a tourist,
to the unsuccessful attempt
of oppression by fascist forces.
I was witness,
even in my naivety,
to the rising of freedom
through human perseverance.
I was witness through this fragile flake
of new understanding
that was painted for me
by the media
many years ago.

Love,
Richard

The Berlin Tourist Trio
We Have Become

Dear Mom and Dad,

We emerged with typical tourist grins
from Wittenberg Platz subway tunnel,
with West Berliner friend
and gracious host Anni Ulich
into the cool light of March
for our first downtown Berlin experience.
We were greeted by a huge silver, rotating
Mercedes symbol atop 40-storey monolith
shining in commercial glory
with modern backdrop of steel and glass.
A bombed-out cathedral
affectionately known
to Berliners as "The Hollow Tooth,"
a towering memorial to WWII,
stands more impressively

than its commercial counterpart.
With craning necks and looks of awe
from here on in, we, for the next 7 days
are the tourist trio from Toronto.

Love,
Richard

The Trip Home to Toronto
over North Atlantic Sea

Dear Mom and Dad,

Hours of clear uneventful sky
flying west from Amsterdam
took us over frigid
North Atlantic calm expanse
of ocean.
Approaching Labrador,
sea ice formed from
horizon to horizon in huge
motionless tectonic plates,
geometric, crystalline desert faces
rounded by wind-thrust collisions.
Plates of ice turned to barren,
treeless landscape
as we headed towards Toronto
over cold, eastern, uninhabited land.
Off in the distance,
gliding over speckled countryside
the crisp shadow of our plane,
in sight from small cabin window
guides the way to home.

Love,
Richard

A Prototype for Perfection

Dear Mom and Dad,

Deutsches Symphonie – Orchester Berlin
March 17, 2000 – 8pm
Andrey Boreyko conducting
– Ludwig van Beethoven
Concerto #5 for Piano and Orchestra op. 73
– Dmitri Shostakowitsch
Symphony #5, op. 47

Francois – René Duchable's ivory performance
a demonstration in gentle perfection.

Andrey Boreyko's energetic, flamboyant
conducting followed by round upon round
of ceaseless applause, bravo, bravo
demanding Boreyko's return.
Four times he emerged
with a gracious bow.

Love,
Richard

Dear Mom and Dad,

We continue to enjoy our stay in Berlin.
We have been here for days
but I finally make the time
to send you these poems.
Hugs from the Berlin
that I never expected to see.

Here are a few poems
that might help you see
what we saw.

Love,
Richard

First Night in Berlin

A gentle mist almost rain
cannot keep us, Berlin visitors
from a late evening stroll
to clear the cobwebs of travel
from weary heads.

Food for Thought

While at the airport watching luggage
snake its way to our plane,
the neighbouring wing tip
was careened into by a catering truck.
Disaster spells delay even for us.
Peanuts and soft drinks must fly
or 100 passengers – us included –
will miss out on KLM's hospitality
but 30-minute delay
is worth smiling about
while protruding truck parts
stick out of wounded wing,
keep other planes on ground
while we are in the air.

Morning Is Rising

Morning is gently rising at 1050 km/hr
from a painful,
sleepless, almost seven-hour flight.
12:40am Toronto time
5:40am sun-time
We fly over jolly old England
Glaswegians' morning alarms are now raising
the workers of life as we jet overhead
past Newcastle, on into Amsterdam.

Now over the remarkably calm
almost whitecapless North Sea
into a pink horizon
past surf-piercing dolphins chasing fishing boats
soon to arch to our destination.
On to Amsterdam past Haarlem
over asphalt black rivers of industrial waste
above asphalt, pinstriped highways
landing on yellow-striped asphalt tarmac.

Pockmarked Reclamation

Touring through Potsdam,
East Berlin,
former Soviet territory,
we were taken back in time
to shredded ceramic building faces'
war-torn evidence of bullet chasings.
Here I was facing the grim truth
of war once again.
Shocked out of my North American naivete
by the preserved evidences of destruction.
The homes of the masses
finally going through
pockmarked reclamation.
Only now after 48 years of peace
since World War II ended,
finally ten years after the celebration
of the tumbling of the Berlin Wall
are they able to return to former glory.

Reclined in the Sun
at the Base of Grunewaldturm

Almost 200 steps to the top
of King William I Tower*
to view Berlin from afar
through whipping wind
and squinting sun.
Spring has not yet risen
from the black March earth of Germany
to block the view with treetops
of distant ancient church spires,
memorials and other sites of interest.
Now back, we wound to the bottom
to recline, on the grass, in the wind-shade calm
in penetrating sun that demands repose.
Holidaying at its best.

Kaiser-Wilhelm-Turm built in 1897

Koenig Wilhelm I Zum Gedaechtniss

*He became the Emperor of all of Germany in 1871 after being King of
Prussia, a neighbouring district in Germany.*

Don't Forget To Stamp
Your Transit Ticket
in Berlin

Green line subway station 11:30am Monday
on our way to Check Point Charlie
to gain a better historical perspective
on the Berlin Wall we had our own standoff
with a seemingly unfriendly intervening transit authority.
With an officious attitude we three were
hoisted from our comfortable subway seat
by a non-English speaking subway official.
Wilful and deliberate body language
dragged us off the train.
Broken English told us, with some difficulty,
that we had not stamped our transit ticket
before boarding the train.
With rules broken we were each in line
for a 60 DM penalty, a hefty fine.
Protests of innocence by ignorance
gesticulations of perplex seemed to go unnoticed.
More officious body language showed us
how to stamp our ticket after kiosk purchase.
Gesticulations became more friendly.
Pointing at his watch told us
that we could use the ticket until 3am.
A wave and a smile had us on our way
without a fine or even harsh warning.
Faith in humanity renewed.

The Hollow Tooth

Up from the concrete of Berlin's central core
protrudes a monument to man's inhumanity to man.
A monument, in my mind, titled
"Destruction and Defeat."
The bombed out shell of
Kaiser Wilhelm Memorial Cathedral,
once a grand, majestic testament
to faith and spiritual progress
now, with tongue in cheek, by Berliners called
The Hollow Tooth.
Now it only half-heartedly points to the sky.
Main building bombed to smithereens,
tip of spire now hollow, empty and decayed.

On first sight I was moved
by the fear that must have torn through
the soul of civilization,
and then as if a calamity

the bells of the new neighbouring church roared
directly overhead, a deafening cacophony of disease.
The hollow clanging bellowed
past my Hollywood-generated imagination
of the horrors of war that bomb down
on innocent heads.

Berlin 2000

A) Reconstruction

New concrete, steel and glass
everywhere you look
over 70 construction cranes
pointing in all directions
from past to future
from mistakes to correction
from beaten to survived
erected over painful past
obliterating too recent oppression
all insight from the gigantic
glass geometric dome
of progress, the Reichstag.*

The wall is down,
buildings are up,
continuous decade of rebirth
redefining Berlin as friendly,
modern superpower
since the fall of the infamous wall.

German Parliament Building

B) History Lesson

Hitler crushed,
Germany defeated in 1945,
four Superpower allies,
USSR, Britain, France and USA,
dividing up the spoils
into quadrants.

1961, the East, under Soviet rule,
the Reds erect
a concrete barrier,
The Berlin Wall,
against fleeing masses
created by Red greed and domination,
oppress or be oppressed,
mine, mine, all mine,
no one shall go in or out

without my permission.
The East shall live or die
as mine but will remain mine.
Grand plan of subjugation falls
with Wall in 1989.

I will show you our pics
when we see you
back in Canada.
For now we send our love.

Your #1 son,
Richard
xx

To Mother

A Bellow Echoed Through My Boyhood

July 10, 2014

Dear Mother,

I was wandering down memory lane today
thinking of father. Four months now since his passing.
I was remembering my teenage years when we all lived
on Erie Avenue, in a two-storey house
with a knee-wall attic filled with stuff. The house
seemed plenty big enough from the outside,
though with two sisters sharing a bedroom,
two brothers and I sharing another down the hall,
Little Grandma in her bedsitting room with a private kitchen
and a boarder in a bed-sit beside the girls' bathroom,
you and dad on the first floor at the back of the house
with a crib for baby Victoria.
One might wonder how we all could fit in.

Our house was large enough that you had to holler.
Small enough that you could be heard from
the distant damp bowels of the basement
all the way to the hot stuffy attic.
"It is my turn in the bathroom"
rang through every corner.
"It is time to leave for school."
"Don't leave your shoes in the hall."
"Who left the toilet seat up?"
These words and more would echo
from the constant chaos of nine people.

Us boys knew we were in trouble
when we heard the thunderous rumble,
a bellow through the ductwork
to every corner of the house.

"Wheeerrrreee is my screwdriver?"
Next week…
"Wheeerrrreee are my pliers?"
Next week…
"Wheeerrrreee is my hammer?"

LOL

How many times would we have to be told
in the same bellowing voice,
though eye to eye at this point,
"Put the tools back where you found them!"
Nothing ever sank in.
The only thing we never missed was
"Come for dinner."

Thinking of you always.

Love you,
#1 son,
Richard
xxoo

Never Ending Love

Transcribed from a Christmas card I wrote
to my 92 year old covid quarantined mother
whom I have not seen for months.
My heart is broken.

December 6, 2020

Dear Dear Mother,

Do you know that I love you
and think of you every day,
many times in a day. You are
never very far from me,
remembering that I was
once a little boy, a child held
in your arms, comforted,
loved, cherished. I thought
that I was
the only one you loved
but then I learned
you had such an abundance of love
that you could give me
your never ending love
and still give
that same love to everyone.
For this I love you forever
for teaching me
what love is all about. I hope
I give you
more than a dot of that love back.

I am still hoping
that we will be able to see you soon
and give you a Christmas kiss from
the bottom of my heart.

Your number one son,
Richard
xxooxxooxxooxxooxxooxxooxxoo

To the Family

Welcome Nico

December 29, 2017

My Dear Nico,

My grandson, only hours old
in terms of terra firma, this
your human existence. Welcome
to this earthly plane.
Is it your penance or your reward
that you landed here, though
through thought and deed
that is for you to determine.
It was wise of you to pick
two loving mothers
that will dote over you,
love you like no one else
possibly could but maybe not
fulfil your every whim.

Nana Kim and I are still in Cuba
but already love you nonetheless
despite the salt wind distance of flailing
palm fronds and pushing waves
into frothing whitecaps.
One day I hope we will walk
these sandy wind-swept shores
of Cuba with you and snooze
under swaying palm-filtered sun.
For now you will have to be content
to be cooed at by mother's love,
gawked at by the many others
that swoon in your presence.

We look forward to meeting you soon.

Grandpa Tai
xxoxxxoxxxoxxxoxxxoxxxoxxxo

In Celebration of Parker's Arrival

May 28, 2021

Dearest Parker,

Welcome to this new exploration,
Love's journey of sights and sounds.
This is the start of an amazing adventure.
Two days ago you arrived into our hearts,
into the late May season of lilacs.
They are so splendid this year;
glorious blooms
in celebration of your arrival.
I am sorry you missed
the sun-yellow smile of daffodils.
They were cheering you on
to come, "Come and join us, dear Parker."
They could not wait but you will see them
next year in their beaming glory.

How God blessed you are
to be born to such wonderful parents.
Congratulations for your fine choice
of whom you will spend your life with.
I predict years of joy-filled love
to and from you.

Looking forward to meeting you soon
even if only in pixel images
until covid lockdown lifts
and you can come to Canada.

Gentle hugs and kisses.

Your Great Uncle Tai and Auntie Kim
xoxoxoxoxoxoxoxoxoxoxoxoxoxoxoxoxoxo

Who Am I but Many

Dear Esme,

I started out life as a son.
I turned simultaneously
into a grandson, a brother,
a cousin and a nephew.
Eventually I became a friend
to one, then many
and then a boyfriend.
I became an uncle to a few,
then a husband
then a father,
an ex-husband and back
to being a husband.
Eventually I became a proud
grandfather
two times over,
grandpa Tai as I am called,
and now I am a first time
great uncle to Esme Anne,
daughter of mother, Kristi
and father, Julian
simultaneously a cousin
and a niece.
I am thrilled for me
and them and Esme.

Love you already,
Great Uncle Tai

To Family and Friends

The Dance

July 10, 2016

Dear Bill, Julie and Josh,

the trees
they danced last night
they danced like they had
never danced before
they danced on that strobe-lit stage
of black and silver
they bowed to the distant audience
on dark and distant hills
before the thunder even came
and then they danced some more
they laughed and swung
their outstretched arms
in unpredicted undulations
they put on such a splendid show
for our standing ovation

hours later
after the performance was done
we sat still on the deck
the woods still trembling, dripping
while the orchestra
faded into the distance.

Wish you were here
at the cabins with us.

Kim and Tai
x

It Should Be Enough

November 20, 2017

Dear Bill, Julie and Josh,

Are you coming out to
our Presqu'ile this weekend?
I was thinking that:

If this view of wind-swept waves, grey,
low-slung clouds
with shafts of dazzling penetrating hope
was all there was for me
to set my gaze upon,
then it would be enough.

If this wild apple tree with gorgeous
fall-puckered apples, Christmas
ornaments glinting in setting sun,
deer candy hanging in reach
was all there was to set my gratitude
into a joyous leap,
then it would be enough.

If this warming, toe-caressing fire,
lulling me to sleep
with crackles of sun sparks
was all there was to be content about
and soothed by,
then it would be enough.

Looking forward to seeing you.

Hugs to you all,
Tai
x

A Walk with Kim

January 12, 2020

Dear Bill and Julie,

Kim and I went for a walk
down to Salt Point this evening.
Last night the silver sky
was clear and calm
with a bright full moon
that shone on sparkling snow
painting deep-blue night shadows
across waning drifts.
Tonight the view is completely different.
The wind blows
over the whispering lake
from the southeast.
Though moonless
the drifting snow glowed
as if the light were lifting
from the frozen ground
more purple than blue.

Ice crystals pelted
our backs and whistled
over our hoods as we slogged
to the point where we met you
for a swim only two months ago.

Our penetrating walk
took us past crashing shore,
tectonic plates pushing
pebbles into groaning mounds,
next year's beach.

These slabs of ice reminded me
of flying over Labrador with Kim and Bill
on our way home from Berlin.
Gosh, what year was that?
We witnessed vast mile upon mile

sheets of ice slowly crashing, crushing
one into the other,
barren land and empty sea
stretching on forever.

Kim and I sat huddled
listening to the wind whipping
through black branches.
We heard our own breath
soughing through our ice encrusted scarves.
A remarkable absence of clucking, swooping
squawking. We were the only beings
walking on this hallowed ground
present and timeless.

Upon our return
ice chafed our faces
as we plodded
through rising
drifts we could only see
inches in front of our frozen stride.

Pressing on we reached
our 'Cuba beach',
as we've fondly named it,
dipping east under naked
arms of weeping willows
stunningly calm there.
The wind blew above our heads
instead of directly into our reddening faces.
We stood and relaxed,
arms linked into arms
for a few minutes
simply relishing the moment
of place and time.

Looking forward to seeing you soon,
Tai

Charles William Sherman

known to family and friends as Bill

August 2013

My Dear Sherman Family,

I was thinking about dad Sherman
again today as I often do.
I was putting away some movies
when it came to mind
that dad joined us
one month for our family and friends'
men's night out to see
the Tom Cruise action-thriller movie
Mission Impossible. I remember
when we were leaving the theatre
all pumped up with cordial camaraderie
after two hours of action-packed stunts –
"Wasn't that something,
at the end of the movie,"
dad said as we walked to the car,
"The helicopter that was flying,
tethered to the train,
through the tunnel."
We were all laughing and carrying on
about the implausibility but
loved it nonetheless.
Dad stopped us and said –
"Which one was Tom Cruise?"
I never knew if he was serious
or was the question
part of his dry sense of humour
that would spring up in the funniest places.

I think his favorite joke
when someone was leaving the house was,
"Here's your hat, what's your hurry."
If I heard him say that once
I heard him say it fifty times.
It's like him saying, *sufficiently suffuncified.*
After a satisfying meal
he would sit back in his chair and say,
"I'm sufficiently suffuncified."
I would smile every time.
I very often think of him fondly.

With Love,
Son-in-law,
Tai

Making Parents Proud
Even Now at 66 in 2020

June 2020

Dear Karen and Cath,

The local paper
will publish my Poet Laureate
Canada Day poem prior to July 1.
It will be sent through ethereal waves,
emailed to me from the editor.
I will print the article, crisp sheets
of white paper folded, lick a stamp
and mail it to our
ninety-two-year-old mother and hope
that a nurse will read it to her
in my covid-dictated absence.

At sixty-six I am still
trying to make her proud,
though no great effort is needed.
I still love her gentle stroke
on my wanting cheek with her cool,
callous-free hands followed by the praise of
"Well done, my number one son."
I will be forever five, proudly presenting her
with a handmade Mother's Day card,
anticipating, expecting, hoping for the stroke
of approval, the tribute of love.

Our dear father,
who is already part of the otherworld,
passed on a few years ago,
will maybe see the video on YouTube
if he is casting his ghostly eye this direction
and send out a puff of praise
from his small brass box,
from where he was interred.

Hugs from covid land of no visits,
Bro
xx

Fragments of Memories

May 10, 2020

Dear Karen and Cath,
my sisters

Mother is living with what is left
of memories, fragments of time
surfing on a milky pool of reality.
It was very cold when skating
with her father, her at twelve
walking when no one else dared
join them at the rink, scattered glimpses
of scarfed faces blurred into focus,
boots almost too cold to put back on,
running home hand in hand with her father.
Now all these years later, knuckles white
gripping wheelchair, running to get warm.
Soft silver hair shadows the recollections
of tobogganing. Was it with her brother
or her children fifty or sixty years ago?
Fragments of memories slip
between pillow and breakfast,
pillow and lunch while gazing
at the undulating shadows,
time playing tricks on the wall.

Hugs from Kim and me.

All the best,
Bro

28th or the 29th

August 18th

Dear Rebecca,

my darling first-born, my stardust.
after saying that
how can i
turn and ask you what is your birthday? ,-)
july 28th or 29th
let me guess – no i won't – i will be wrong.
it is not for lack of love that i forget
it is not a lack of interest or fondness
it is not a lack of wonderment
or awe at your creativity,
spark of life or generous smile,
it is a lack of synapses that fire properly.
i love you whether you were
born on the 28th or the 29th
but my calendar cares
and so should i.

hugs,
your ever forgetful father
xxoo

Of Dust

May 29, 2017

Dear Theo,

Go my friend.
Go to Cyprus and bring back
some celebratory poems about
land and
place and
time and
age and
blood and
being.
Bring your grandfather back with you
in poems,
in a jar of ashes,
in memory
or sitting beside you on a seat.

I will not bother changing the e-poster.
I will not tell anyone
about you not coming until I am on stage
and will announce
the kind heart of your absence
and tell them about your
102 year old grandfather –
I will remind them of the importance
of love and blood. I will, or someone will,
read a couple or a few of your poems
in your sad, conspicuous absence
as we celebrate the life of 102.
May you live to that age and beyond
into unwritten poems.

I just talked to my mother,
I call each day, she is 89.
She is well and happy.
If, I guess I should say, when I lose her
I will give up a poetry reading
to be beside her still cold side.

We will talk much later
about a Northshore book launch
of your book in Kingston.
There is lots of time for that.
No Hurry, No Worry.

All is well,
Tai

Blown by the Breeze of Resilience

June 5, 2021

Dear Anna and Tony,

I so, sooo wish,
wish beyond wishes,
we could have tea
in your garden or ours
and bask
in the floral view
with sun-lapped
heavy-headed peonies
bowing to our appreciation.
Fading phlox winking
at our gratitude
scattering
their pink and white confetti
sprinkled
to bridal green lawn.

i wish, i wish,
i hope, i hope
this will happen
sometime sooner than later
after the cloud of covid
is blown
by the breeze of resilience
into fading nothingness.

Tai

Life IS Eternal,
I Hope You Can Trust

Dear Friend,

I heard the news
of your grandson's suicide
from our mutual dear friend.
I am in tears of sorrow
for the loss of your grandson,
for you and for your entire family.
His hidden pain
must have been immense.
I know how much he meant to you.
I am sooooo sorry for your loss.

My palpable grief shudders
to my core
to think that any one of the universe's angels
could be in so much pain
that they think there is only one way forward.
My heart goes out to you and to him.

Life is eternal. I hope you can trust
that he is on his way
to finding a better place free of pain.

With love and compassion,
my deepest condolences,

Tai

Mastered Brilliance

For Laurence Hutchman on receiving his poetry book
Swimming Toward the Sun *published by Guernica Editions*

November 30, 2020

Dear Laurence,

did i thank you yet
as i should have
for the fine fine book
that i pulled
from my glowing mailbox
poetry spilling
into the covid quiet lobby.

i opened the bulging
book-heavy packet
to find your smile of joy
greeting me
on your poetic path of life.

your generosity leapt
into voice by Kim
reading to me
as we crept onto the highway
to leave the covid city
of toronto to our dot of heaven
in the quietude of presqu'ile.
your poems warmed the way
ploughing through time
like the cooing of a dove
on a mist-filled morning.

thank you Laurence
for spending the years
to bring us
your crafted words
of mastered brilliance.

Hugs from Kim and Tai

Late October Afternoon

After Laurence Hutchman

Dear Laurence,

Hear the last leaves of fall,
clinging,
to the shimmer of autumn.
The ground covered,
trees half bare.
Smell the amber dampness
in the pale cool air of tomorrow.

Thank you for your poems,
Tai

In This We Call Now

For Ellen Jaffe

November 17, 2021

Dear Ellen,

Hang in there sweet poet
and keep on writing.
Your words will carry you
past this now to the next now
as ours will for all of us.
We will all write our last poem
sooner or later. We all have to learn
the lesson of living in the now,
writing our last poem
over and over again.
Sweet friend, we will all live
in the now of each poem, the now
between the poems, the now
that writes the poem, the now
that is the poem.

All I can do is send my love now
and know that you are the poem
of now, the poem of eternity.

Hugs,
Tai

Having a Great Time
with Warm Feet

For poet friend Don Gutteridge

February 13, 2021

Dear Don,

I was working on the layout
of your new book today –
it is always a pleasure
to work with your fine poetry
but it is time to get up
from the landscape
of my desk and monitor
and move the body. In these
silly covid times Kim and I
are well
cocooned in our own offices
working away but we will get out
for a walk in this mid-month
chill of February – only weeks
before our memories
of warmer times are rejuvenated.
We try to get out once a day,
otherwise the body will cramp up
or wither away. An hour walk
in the wind at -13°C,
in our Ontario "damp" cold,
is sometimes too much
though it reminds me
of my winter camping days
in the mountains of Banff
when I worked as an oven cleaner
at the Banff Springs Hotel.
Rolled oats, a pot, sleeping bag,

no tent for a week at a time
up Bow River into wilderness.
No footprints there
except for wolf, fox and elk,
maybe a scampering rabbit
or slithering river otter
not interested in eating me.
Those were the hardy days
of skiing into the wilderness
all on my own. Those camping days
are long past
but they make for great memories.
Now two inches from seventy
I am at my desk where I languor
in the past having a great time
with warm feet.

As I finish typing this email to you
I realize I am listening to Springsteen's
"Glory Days"
filling my head from ear-hugging headphones
that I did, and am, now living the glory days.
This album harkens back to 1984 –
37 years ago, not all that long
after my Banff adventure years.
Time flies when you are having fun
basking in memories while publishing books.

I trust you are well in your lockdown –
staying safe, sound and happy.

With "warm" regards,
Tai
x

In the Eye of a Whale

for David Swanger

September 27, 2021

Dear David,

OMG – amazing pic of you.
Black hump of a whale
diving under your kayak.
Ashamed of this uninspired cliché
all I can say is "Amazing."
You are so God blessed
to have been
in the eye of a whale
saying hello.

25 years ago I was in arm's reach
of a Right Whale sailing
in the Atlantic with buddy Barry
on his 55 foot gaff cutter.
Mainsail taut against stiff winds,
storm jib only half unfurled,
listing, dumping gusts
from furrowed brow.
Port gunnel dipped
into teeming ocean,
my arm splashing leaping surf
when out of the green abyss
glided the black glisten
of a snorting whale. My instinct
was to pull back out of fear.
If I had been prepared
I could have caressed
his ebony gleaming back.

Your photo
splashed me back
to that July moment.
Thank you.

All the best,
dry-landed smiling,
Tai

A collaborative found poem between
Glen Sorestad and Richard Grove/Tai

What Canadians Talk About the Most

February 8, 2021

Dear Tai,

Spring
may be just around the corner,
but this morning
as I was making coffee at 7:30a.m.
the weather was beastly –
the actual temperature was -38°C,
with the wind chill
it was an unbelievable -54°C.
We will not
be poking our noses outside
to test the severity of it.

Glen

Dear Glen,

I once lived in Calgary.
As the saying goes –
if you fall on the ice
on your way to the car
and no one finds you
you could die.
At those temperatures
not even the vultures
would be able to peck
at your frozen body.
It sometimes
got down to -45°C
The tires on the car

would be frozen flat
on the bottom. It would take
15 minutes of driving
to bring them back to round.

Stay warm and safe,
Tai

Dear Tai,

Sadly, it's true
when you get wind chills
in excess of -50°C you are
in the danger zone.
It is conceivable that should you
fall outside and not be noticed
for even a half-hour,
you could die, though several hours
unnoticed would almost guarantee it.

Even if you dress in the warmest
clothes possible, any exposed flesh
will freeze almost in a matter of seconds
when the wind chill
temperature sinks into the -50s.
Just breathing in air that cold
for a matter of minutes would
be enough to hospitalize anyone
whose respiratory system
may be compromised.

We take this kind of cold very seriously.
We'll avoid going out – willingly
– into that kind of cold.

Glen

Covid Restrained Love

December 6, 2020

Dear Graham and Stella,

Kim and I send out
covid restrained love
wishing we could drop in
and see you, but for now
we have to wave
over the internet
with our unending affection
for you both.
It is so important
that you are kept safe and sound
in these restricted times.

Hugs from us both,
Tai
xo

Celebrating Life

February 8, 2021

Dear Anna,

Thank you for the pics of your
deep Quebec snow,
Tony pushing a wheelbarrow
of firewood.
You have way more snow,
pristine,
than we have here. We still have
tufts of grass peeking out
from October's mowed lawns,
no accumulation.

I love the pic of your front door.
It is so inviting. I wish
I could stomp the snow from my feet
on the inside of your warm vestibule
and come in
for a cup of tea
across your kitchen table –
even without a mask if needed.

-13°C is cold enough for me
but we gathered with family
for a covid parka party
in a park for chocolate cake
with candles – Lionel's
belated birthday celebration.
We all signed a card to my mom.
The ink in the pen was frozen.
I had to warm it inside my coat.
Nothing is going to stop us
from celebrating Life.

Hugs from our Toronto condo,
Tai
xx

Billowed Back to Life

for John B. Lee

March 26th, 2016

Dear John,

A few days ago we had a stupendous ice storm.
Everything was covered with an inch of ice.
Trees were bowing in submission
to their now shining branches.
The car was a glistening ice sculpture.
Against my apparent better judgment
I went out for a walk and slipped
on the ice. Picture this blue bear,
as my dear sister Adonay calls me, flying in the air
with winter boots horizontal
three feet off the ground
landing square on my back followed by
my coconut head
breaking the ice a frozen moment later.
I rolled to my side gasping. 10 seconds,
15, 20 seconds passed
before I could bring a breath of life
back into my collapsed lungs.
In those 20 seconds
I thought I was going to perish
without saying thank you for your poems. My lungs
billowed back to life as I lay
on the frozen road.
Kim paralyzed, helpless, praying.

When you are trying to stand back up
after a sack-of-potato fall like this
in the middle of a frozen road,
there is nothing to hold on to
but God's wing.
I shimmied, danced and skated myself
back to my six feet, two inch view of the world.
That is a long way for a bulk like me to land
without a runway or parachute.

In contrast, today, only a day later
I was out working in the garden.
I just came in from doing some winter cleanup
in the front flower beds – raking and pulling
dead plants from the sun-bathed earth,
though ice is still disappearing in the shade
under the bushes on the north side of the house.
It is a sunny, gorgeous +14°C, no ice on the road,
not a cloud in the sky – tonight promises to be +3°C.
I was working in short sleeves,
wiping sweat from my brow as I dug.
How wonderful it is to be digging.
How wonderful it is to be able to dig.

All the best,
Tai

Patience Has Her Perfect Work

for Brian Ostrander, distinguished Mayor of Brighton
(the title is from James 1,4-8 KJV*)*

October 12, 2018

Dear Brian,

Congratulations Brian Ostrander.
Maybe no landslide victory for you,
but your cool calm demeanour,
your persistence over years,
your hotly debated issues
have won you your deserved title of
Mayor Ostrander of Brighton, Ontario
by just over 100 votes,
a 3.5% nail-biting conquest.

Patience has her perfect work,
bringing a new era of congeniality
to the council floor
marked with forward moving progress
on more than just the platform
of outdated strategic plans and
water management fiasco.

With your victorious five council,
all good people,
may you move mountains
with Brighton's future
firmly held in your velvet-glove
leadership model.

Citizen Tai

In the Lap of My Dentist

September 1, 2021

Hi John,

All is well.

Sorry I did not take
your call earlier,
cell phone singing
in my breast pocket,
un answered.
I was upside down
with my head
in the lap of my dentist,
staring
into the nostrils
of his fine-complexioned assistant.

Forty-five minutes and
almost $800 later I am home,
lip throbbing,
wallet throbbing.
They give a senior's discount
but not
a poet laureate discount.

After such a neck-strained
appointment, mouth yanked
to one side like a speckled trout
suspended by piercing hook,
blue fingers fidgeting,
suction tub slurping at my
metallic saliva,
I need a massage therapy session
for my neck and one for my wallet.

I should have taken my new
Black Moss Press poetry book
and traded it even-steven
for the dental work.
A lifetime of poetry for his
dedicated life
of looking into the abyss of
pearl-lined caverns.

Your lip-thawing friend,
the clueless poet, for they pulled
the last of my wisdom teeth
ages ago.

Tai

Levitation

For John B. Lee and the definition of pricks, thorns and barbs

Dear John,

Four feet is a long way to fall
landing bum first into a thorny bush.
The pricks or thorns or barbs,
whatever you might call them,
cat-clawed me, trapped me,
so that I could not move. To rescue
myself by simply standing up meant
a million daggers, clawing, scratching,
gouging at my back, my neck, my legs.
The backs of my hands and arms
were already bleeding. Even relaxing
while I contemplated my exit strategy
was painful while droplets of life
dripped to the garden below, staining
the alabaster lilies that reached up
to touch my thorn-throbbed self.
Levitation with the help of five co-workers
was my God-sent salvation.
Standing shirtless they pulled
the devil claws from my back,
from my shredded buttocks.
Still able to laugh we all returned
to finishing the roofing job we had started.

Always good to share my stories with you.

Tai

Numbers

November 24, 2020

Dear John,

hugs to you and Cathy in Port Dover
outside of the lockdown area.
i trust all is well with you both –
missing you.
it looks like we are, full-fledged,
into a more solid covid lockdown
in the known universe,
Toronto and Peel Region.
that sure covers a lot of geography
including Mississauga, Brampton,
all the way north to Orangeville,
east to Pickering.
some of the lockdown rules
seem silly to me but as a
disobedient kind of authority-rebelling
kind of guy i am i will do my best
to obey the lockdown until
the prescribed December 21.
let's hope the numbers shift to the better
and we can see you soon.

as always, be covid safe.
all the best to your fam.

Tai
x

Resurrection

April 27, 2017

Dear John,

I could not help myself.
I had to write a poem,
no matter how morbid,
about your experience witnessed
by Manuel. I am glad I was not there,
I wish I was there –
undecided morbidity swells
in my imagination,
so here is my poem inspired
by your and Manuel's recollections.

Tai
x

A Post Easter Resurrection

A friend died on his floor. Yes
literally died. Head bashed, hanging
on baseboard, limp,
a greying-white ghost. Yes
literally, collapsed, widow mourning
her loss in hysteria, no pulse,
no verbose emanations
or tolerated, garrulous expositions passed
his blue lips, though now he is still alive,
resurrected, driver's license reinstated,
but yes
it is true he did die. You can ask him.

Now my friend, the witness
to the dark tunnel of death,
a speck of light in the distance,
is brought back to life,
plugged into blinking instrumentation
and forced to cut out junk food,
at least for a few days
or until he dies again.
The doc says – healthy as a horse,
fit as a fiddle – relieved.
Dying seems to have done him
the world of good.

My witness friend's dog
is doing much better too
after a visit to the vet. The vet's bill
almost killed my witness friend,
my friend, that is,
not the dog.

How precarious an existence
do we ramble in our zigzaggy
perilous journey, from
I won or lost at the lottery, to waiting
for another publisher's rejection slip.

I will help rebuild his front steps
and have a yawning
post-carpentry soak
in his hot tub and longing gaze
in his hot tub and long
for migrating birds to arrive
as we sit and wait
for our own resurrection.

Stay well and don't die sooner
than rotations around the sun require.

Tai

Leaping from 2018 into 2019

For Manuel and Adonay, John and Cathy

My Dear Distant by Miles Family,

Here we are stepping into 2019.
The only sad thing about having one foot planted
in 2018 with the other tap dancing its toe
into 2019 is that you will only be in our thoughts.
Miles separate our bodies from hugging
as the chimes of hope and expectation,
goodwill to all mankind, leap from yesterday
into the now of the future
all in one passionate countdown. You will,
all four of you, be with us in spirit
as we embrace another glorious year
of moving forward and feeling, once again,
God blessed. We can thank divine Spirit – God –
for that leap. Thank you, divine Love,
that we have not had any challenges
greater than we can handle. Compassion blended
with nostalgia sticks as a lump in my throat
as I remember dear people like you
that should still be with us. I thank God
that you can still receive emails
of goodwill and courage, love and camaraderie.
I understand that there is no email on the other side.

I love you,
Hugs from Kim and me

Skiing at the Tender Age of
Twelve or Thirteen on the Farm
Behind the Barn on the Hill
in the Back Forty

for John B. Lee because
he also lived on a farm
when he was young

Dear John,

On the farm
when I was just a young lad
at the adventurous age of twelve or thirteen
I strapped on my mother's skis,
curve-tipped wooden slabs
with spring-loaded bindings,
antiques in my mind,
fastened to my green lace-up rubber boots.
The tumble to the bottom of the hill
was a short lived flurry of hilarity.

All the best,
Tai

The Red Eyed Devil Snake

for John B. Lee

01/01/2020

Dear John,

Happy New Year to you and Cathy.
Hugs to you both.
We wish we could pop over for tea
on our way to the store for bread
or a new paint brush
in preparation of painting
the newly hung door
in my new condo office.
Mr. Google says
it is one hour and forty-one minutes
to tea at the Lee's via 401, QEW and #6.
I think she is naive
and does not account for the notorious
Toronto traffic that one has to
contend with. The red-eyed devil snake
that slithers to, through and from
the Big Stink. I would expect
over two and a half hours
before we would have our feet
under your table sipping tea and jawing
about how high the water is going to be
in the spring of 2020.
Hi to Serge.
I hope he gets his dream bone
soon in the new year and like us two-legs
gnarls on his wishes and hopes for a long while.

Hope to see you soon,
Tai

Under the Clock at Union Station

for John B. Lee

October 25, 2020

Dear John,

We decided to meet
tomorrow at noon
under the clock at
Union Station on Front Street.
You will be laden with books,
title upon title of your genius,
words spun from the magic
of your spinning top
tapped from fingers, churned
into white winged books
of contemplation. There
under the ticking of time,
the tick tock of blind arms,
your agile mind will have seen
and absorbed enough material
for ten poems before green
has blinked to red and I pull up
in my petroleum chariot
to whisk you to the reading
in Kensington Market
where you will regale us with
your silver tongue of brilliance.

See you soon,
Tai

Your Pinkletink

for John B. Lee and his pinkletink cover I was working on

June 14th, 2020

Dear John,

I have sore fingers
and wrinkles on my arms
from falling asleep
in front of the computer
with interlocked fingers
listening to the Jan Stirling Trio,
jazz piano, bass and drums from BC.
It was only when
the melodic tickling of the ivories
changed in my i-tunes album shuffle
to Duke Ellington's album
Black, Brown and Beige
did I wake
from my neck-cricked slumber
stared at
by your pinkletink.

Tai

Arrived and Waiting
at Restaurant
while Kim Ducks
into Shop

a text message to
John and Cathy Lee

December 9, 2021

Arrived
Snoozing
Reclined in
Black Mazda
Kim shopping
Every opportunity
Dollar store presents
Still have to be bought

No Hurry No Worry
See you soon
Waiting Tai
Hugs
xx

i will not go to my grave voluntarily
for John B. Lee

December 27, 2021

Dear John,

thank you for your poem
and for always keeping me
in your thought
and on your list of poetry friends.

nice poem
many nice thoughts and ideas —
i like,

> *how it holds you*
> *as the water*
> *is held by the vase*
> *think of the brilliance*
> *of stars*
> *in a well*

wonderful!

you and Cathy are often
fondly in our thoughts
even though we have neglected you
over the last year or two.
covid is my excuse.
busyness and covid-sucked time,
me leaning into the blue glow
of my computer monitor
trying to do more than what time
and finger tapping will allow,

or is it finger tapping busyness
with the excuse of computer-hunched,
covid-cocooning solitude-filled time
or is it the ticking of time
with the frantic desire
to make up for my frolicking
ill-spent youth
and dope clouded
non-literary younger-self years
that i am now paying for
thinking that i will not
go to my grave voluntarily
until i have written a better poem,
better than the last one,
better than the percolating unwritten one
that may never spill
to the still snow-white page of fear.

we hope you had a very Merry Christmas
and have stayed in the peace of 2021
as we linger with fingers poised
to flip the calendar
to the unknown covid dance of 2022.

forever cocooning,
Kim and Tai
xo

Today, Tomorrow, Yesterday

May 19, 2021

Dear John and Cathy,

Mother, at ninety-three,
seems to be doing very well
though she flounders
in her private sense of timelessness.
She slips between now and then,
might be and might have been
without a blink or worry.
She thought that I had been there
two days in a row but was glad
to see me none the less
even though it had been a week.

Today, tomorrow, yesterday
it all does not matter to her
wandering sense
of time and space because
I will forever be her little Ricky
when I walk into her
often shrouded-snoozing room.

She said that my little sister Catharine
had phoned yesterday,
how many yesterdays
she is not sure and she had
no idea of how long
the nice yellow flowers had been there,
sent with love from both sisters –
they just appeared one day and
have been smiling back at her
since their mysterious arrival.

The orchid that I took last week
she thought was a fake plant
from Christmas but with covid
we had no gathering five months ago,
not even a hug.
She will forever be my darling mother,
so grateful for every little thing
including the robin on the window ledge
that was there to sing just for her.
She beamed with gratitude.
I was sad to see
how sad she was when it flew away.

All the best,
Tai

Test Your Fear

February 10, 2021

Dear Manuel and John,

I am up early at my computer this morning.
I woke up to pee at 4:30am.
The sun is not even close to winking
over the horizon yet
but as you know, once the mind is in action
it is hard to turn it off. The blackness
made me think about the sun
shining again in a few hours and the trust
we have that it will.
It takes about eight and a half minutes
for light to reach the earth from the sun.
Almost eight and a half minutes of bliss
before eternal darkness, endless black,
if it were to turn off like a light bulb
and blanket your life. As for the stars,
Google says it takes over 4 years
for the light to reach us from Proxima Centauri
and two and a half million years
from Andromeda Galaxy.
That is kind of far
for the light to get to the earth.
Close your eyes
for just eight and a half minutes,
open them and see if the sun
is shining in your part of the world
or did it turn out when your eyes were closed.
Try it and rejoice in the glory
that the sun still shines. Try it.
we are never afraid that the sun will burn out
while you were contemplating eternal darkness.
It is not much of a test of our fear,

close your eyes for ten minutes,
for thirty or sixty minutes. Each time
if the sun still shines rejoice
in its seeming eternality.
It is still black here but I know
when I open my eyes you will still be here.

bro

To Basu in India

A Delight

November 24, 2020

Dear Basu,

as blurry eyed
and tired as i am tonight
i finished reading
your poetry book.
it truly was a delight

even though
in a haste to go to bed –
midnight barking at my heals –
i managed to tap out
a quick review of your book –
see attached.
i hope it is worthy
of your fine work.
i hope you find a use for it.

if you send me the cover
of your book
i will post the review
on my facebook.
save me a copy
for when we finally meet.
i want a hug and a copy.

all the best,
tai

A Morning in the Park with You

August 2, 2021

Dear Basu,

As always
I think of you
on the other side of the world,
probably asleep.
On some mornings
I visit my local park,
half a block from your condo,
with a coffee and a granola bar
to start my day
and bask in the glory
that finds me there.

Talk to you again tomorrow,
Tai

Scratch Marks a Reminder of His Visit

I have little scratch marks up and down my legs.
A pint-sized friendly black squirrel
visited me in the quiet solitude
in my sun-filled-park morning. At my feet
he did his tentative squirrel-type dance of hesitation
looking up to me wondering when
and what I might feed him. With no food
all I could offer him
was a reciprocal joy-filled moment. He put his little
black-clawed paw on my bare toe. I didn't budge.
After a moment he climbed my leg and sat on my lap,
front paws clenched together praying
that I might have something for him. In a flash
he was gone carrying his unfulfilled expectations
to a nearby tree where he nibbled on maple keys.
With a smile I left the gentle scratch marks on my leg
as a reminder of his visit.

Face Clasped Ecstasy

I sat with outstretched sunbathed legs,
Birkenstocks kicked to the side, watching
a smiling joy-filled mother with her teetering toddler
discovering a mist of water
spraying on his face from playground fountain.
Mother's face-clasped ecstasy watched
this assertation of glee.

His Exuberance and Skill

A young man, maybe twenty-two or so,
was shooting hoops alone. A throbbing echo
filled the park as he threw his joy-propelled ball
through cloudless sky to orange waiting hoop.
With a near silent whoosh, hoop entered,
ball drops into his waiting arms
of fulfilled expectation. On his departure
from now silent court, I thanked him
for his exuberance and skill
that entertained me during
my lazy morning prayers.

     *   *   *

In a few hours you will awake
and fill your day
with your own joy-filled moments
of being the loved of Love,
the purpose-filled expression of divine Soul.

With divine Spirit's commitment
I send my love,
Tai
xx

End of Spring

June 21, 2021

Dear Basu,

I am in Presqu'ile
counting my calm silent moments
by the hour, by the minute
not by the day. It is Sunday, June 21.
The last day of spring
yawns its way into summer
past the rose laden arbour
pompously posing in the backyard.
Arms of pink drape
under the weight of bee-bustled blooms.
Baby robins have already fledged
their nest and chirp their gratitude –
I sing because I can sing.

A dazzlingly red cardinal swoops
into the summering green
of corkscrew willow
that drapes over budding daylilies.
It stops there for a long moment
to pose for my mind-swelled breath.
I sit motionless
becoming a log, a bush. I become stillness.
Only my joy races up and down branches
between still leaves of ponderance.
Cardinal wings to blue
as a flutter of orange glides into view,
branch bows to purple clematis
clinging to ancient wrought iron trellis.

My dear friend,
thank you for joining me for tea, you in India,
me in the heaven called Presqu'ile.

Love,
Tai
xx

Epic Cocooning

November 12, 2020

Dear Basu,

Here I am in Canada
halfway around the world
in the northern hemisphere
thousands of miles from you
in Jamshedpur, India.
Our Canadian autumn is upon us
with frost in the air on some mornings,
north of Lake Ontario,
north of Toronto,
north of the 401 Highway
frost and snow every day.

With the mesmeric fear of covid
and winter hovering,
Kim and I are ready for
an epic cocooning at the condo.

From our fourth floor window
facing northeast we have the very last
Maple leaf hanging, clinging
to the memory of warmer days
shimmering on branch, black.

A grey-squirrel's face stuffed full of autumn
looks for a place to build her nest.
A blanket of winter hovers,
pushing her to hunker down.
The smell of amber dampness lingers
in the thin cool air of
wishing it were warmer.

Hugs from Canada,
Love Tai

Happy New Coming In

December 31, 2020, 8:50pm

Dear Basu,

Here I am, knocking at your door
once again for a cup of Indian chai tea.
You always open your door to me
and welcome me in. The kettle is always hot.
I always try to bring a special cookie or cake.
What a wonderful friend you have become,
what a wonderful friend you are. Thank you.
In such a short time I can say I love you.
You are one of few
for whom I carefully use that word.
My dear sisters Adonay and Michelle,
their husbands, my brothers,
Manuel and Jorge in Cuba,
John and Cathy sharing a different
ocean-size lake. Thank you
for sharing your lit life with me, your poems,
your readings, your books but also
for sharing other parts of who you are
that one shares only with a true friend.

Today I shared some pics of my
Presqu'ile walk in the woods.
You are always the first,
pics of the last sunset, snow in my beard.
What makes this last sunset of 2020 so special?
The first of 2021 might be just as glorious,
the fifth, the twentieth will all be different
and splendid, but the last
has a melancholy note that sings of finality.
The year did not just fade out

with a droll or witless blur but died out
with an almost vulgar sizzle as it dipped
into the lake, setting
into a grey abyss as it deserved.

I would say, have a great rest of 2020
in these last few hours but I am sure
you are sound asleep well into your dreams
of 2021 – always 10.5 hours
ahead of me in Ontario. Kim and I
had a nice dinner in front of the tv
with headphones on
so we didn't bother our B&B guests upstairs.
For now I am at my computer in my office,
Kim at hers at the dining room table.
We will meet for a New Year's tea
sometime soon.

For now I have to say I am fading fast.

Hugs from this side of the big blue marble.

With love,
Tai
xxoo

I Scramble with You

January 4, 2021

Dear Basu,

I am trying to find a funny way to say
that I scramble with you. On my phone
I see that there is a poem from you
so I scramble to open it while Kim is in the store.
She is much too quick
so I don't get to read much more than
a couple of enticingly-interesting lines.
As I scramble to close out of phone email
I see that you have left a second email,
that I scramble to open,
in the twenty or thirty seconds
while groceries are plunked into the back-hatch
of our car – I should have been helping.
All I manage to see is your smile
in a couple of lines. Off goes my phone.
We are back on the highway
heading back to the condo from Presqu'ile.
I hear your email whispering to me the entire trip.
I have put the second load of weekend laundry
in the washer already and I have sent a quick reply
to an email from my brother Christopher
and then I scramble to open your emails
but by then I really don't have much time for tea
with you as it is already 6pm and other demands
are mounting, a snow drift
as beautiful as it is can hardly be stepped over,
keeping me from your always generous words
but then again I guess it does not matter all that much
considering your pillow is still warm
and your scramble of feeding children and rushing

off to teach will not start for hours.
I will make my way to you
in a calmer manner later. For now
we will both have to dance the wordless,
solo dance of scramble.
See you soon.

Hugs,
Tai
xo

Orange Hug

March 31, 2021

Good morning Dear Basu,

7:45am sitting on the side of the bed,
birds are perched in our tree singing
even though it is a grey rainy day.
I am a bit blurry-eyed still
but had a good night's sleep,
best in a while.
Had some strange indescribable dreams
of swirling colours,
art that swam over me and buildings.
It is as if it were alive,
filling my entire being.
Have a great day
in the colours of your today.
Here is an orange hug.

All the best,
Tai

Nothing To Do with Jimi Hendrix –
"Purple haze all around,
don't know if I'm
coming up or down..."

Saturday August 29, 2021

Dear Basu,

As always, I am thinking of you in India.

Kim and I are in Presqu'ile.
We had a gathering last night
that we call the "Fireside Poetry Reading."
Ten of us this year for a casual poetry reading.
Our 20th annual.
Some years we have had many more
and other years fewer.

This evening, the day after,
the sky is stained with purple low-hung clouds
with thunder rattling in the thick hot air.
It will rain soon.

In the still hour of 3am
lightning split the sky jagged.
A deluge of cats and dogs danced
on our metal roof. A joyous sound
of rejuvenation
after many days of powdered earth
sucked dry by 30°C full sun.
Today the sky is a calm blue
with few clouds, leaves are rustling
in a gentle 20°C breeze of gratitude.

We hear of your river-swelling
monsoon season.
Stay dry, my dear friend.

Tai
xx

spring is trying

March 6, 2021

Dear Basu,

it is a grey Saturday morning here in Toronto
with a slight wisp of snow
that swirls defying gravity,
disappearing as it slowly hovers
landing on child's eager out-stretched tongue.
Spring is trying hard to arrive. During the day
it shows up with confidence and certainty,
temperatures poised
at the thermometer's red line mark of zero,
a soaring vulture hovering, scanning for death.
At night the temperature
swooped down to -13°C to peck at death's remains,
screeching like a red-tailed hawk, screaming
that winter is not over as he flies off
with talon-pierced prey,
the snowploughed banks still solid,
slowly dwindling, gravel-speckled boulders
balking the inevitable. The hidden snow
in the shadowed recesses
under low-slung branches resists
the rising daytime temperatures.
There is no life in newly exposed
dog-pooped grass
but it always seems to come back –
the resilience of life.
Even the long-trod paths
of muddied shortcut
will eventually green into summer's arrival.

I hope that you are
enjoying the arrival of your spring.

Hugs from Canada,
Tai
xx

Squeezing Air

October 23, 2020

Dear Basu,

I had a visit from my back-seat grandson
on a dreary-grey-drizzling afternoon.
He wanted a hello and a goodbye hug.
How can you break the heart
of a six-year-old and tell him
no
it is not safe in these covid-fear-filled times
of an invisible threat,
a hovering manifestation of man's mind,
with mass hysteria, that I cannot hug him.
From the front seat I showed him
a six-foot-distant hug
where I squeezed the air
with my grandpa arms and sent
a smile past my mask
that reached his heart.
With a smile back from his dove-cooing eyes
he squeezed the air,
tighter and tighter, face flushed, arms quaking.
His mother, my darling daughter,
laughed and said, don't hurt Grandpa Tai.
Don't squeeze too hard.
With spilling sorrow,
he loosened his bear-hug air-grip and hugged
with the most gentle caress
as one might hug a kitten.
Sorry Grandpa Tai. I love you.
Walking away from the car
he turned towards me and sent
a quick gentle air hug and a tender smile
that almost broke my heart.

This covid thing is sometimes tough to handle.

Hugs from Canada,
Tai

Stroke and Nourish

November 26, 2020

Dear Basu,

It is always my pleasure
to share emails with you
halfway around this
growing-smaller-and-smaller world.
I found your email on my phone
this morning, the first thing
that I looked at before
I even got out of bed. You,
so many miles away just retiring –
me foggy brain just waking
to the new day of blessings –
you my first. One day
we will have to meet, at least on zoom,
as we can't meet for coffee,
it would be cold by the time I got there.
By the way, just in case
one day we do meet for coffee,
I drink decaf.

I am sorry to hear
about your bereavement.
In these lockdown times
it is even sadder. We can't be
with the ones we love, the ones
that stroke and nourish us or vice-versa,
the ones that need us
to stroke and nourish them.

I have a long day ahead of me
surrounded by poetry in every direction –
much of it the boring
administration stuff but it has to be done.

With warm hugs,
Tai

teleportation skills

December 18, 2020

Dear Basu,

even though with tongue in cheek
i am starting to dislike
time and geography.
they are both against me.
there are not enough hours in the day
and i don't have
my teleportation skills down pat
for me to blink my eye,
tap my heels together
and arrive at your door
to beg a cup of Indian chai tea
and press for a hug.

i am so grateful
that you are feeling perfectly better.
i did not stop praying for you,
knowing your inviolable perfection.
thank the divine that prayer
knows nothing about time and geography —
only unbroken perfection.

i have been busy in time and space as usual.
sometimes too busy for my own good.
it feels like days since i talked with you
but the sun tells me it is much less than that.
we need to start working on a plan
for me to come to your university, humbly
to give a workshop/s on writing poetry.
i need an economic excuse
to push me to your door
knowing the kettle will be on.

as always,
love,
Tai

today, tomorrow or yesterday

June 10, 2021

Dear Basu,

Is it today, tomorrow or yesterday in India?
What time does the dark dream
of this endless pandemic start and stop.
Does your past, present or future
come before or after mine in Ontario.
I have such a hard time keeping track
of the earth spinning around the sun
at gargantuan speeds, unfathomable,
you on one side of this big blue marble,
me on the other, simultaneous yawns
of waking and sleeping. Rubbing eyes
at the same time, pillow hot, pillow cold,
hungry for life, hungry for sleep. A poem
streams from finger-tapping keys
tumbling into dreams.

For a week we had 30+°C you at 40+.
I do hope you have a/c to help
keep you smiling with your kids and husband
at your covid lockdown dinners. For me,
I am just at my computer, working, working,
publishing, writing, sleep, eat and a bit of TV
between more writing, sleeping, eating.

Basically all is well here
on the sunny side of the earth creeping
into the dark of another tomorrow. I trust
all will be well with you as you wake
to watch, to use your words,
your "parents withering in this pandemic"
watching the hourglass drain
the sands of time over their patient quietude,
a quickening river
on the way to their endless horizon.

Hugs from Canada,
Tai
x

The Joy of Now

March 3, 2021

Dear Basu,

It is 8am and the sun is shining
glorious,
streaming in, across our windowsill
filled with twelve or fifteen smiling plants,
spilling the joy of now across the wall,
lapping, warming more than halfway
into the apartment. Every corner
is filled with love. Even at this moment
at my computer, in my small windowless office
light reaches even under my desk.
If the penetrating sunlight can reach every corner
then so can God's love for you
reach every dark crevice of thought,
extinguishing all fear.

Sit and be still with me for a few moments today –
    "Be still and know that I am God."
Know with me that divine Love is taking care of you.
    "...they that wait upon the Lord
shall renew their strength;
they shall mount up with wings as eagles;
they shall run, and not be weary;
and they shall walk, and not faint."

I smell from a distance that my coffee is now made;
my toast has popped ready
for my peanut butter and jam.

With a bounty of hugs,
Tai
xx

Your Now Darkening Side
of This Planet We Call Earth

December 1, 2020

Dear Basu,

Through the vertical blinds of our bedroom,
slats of a grey morning yawn
over our still sleeping, blanketed figures,
Kim's and my lifeless lumps of slumber.
6:30am is too early to rise
to face the demands of a busy day
considering I went to bed at 1:30am
after working on the layout and design
of a dear poet's book.

An electronic Jamaican jingle
dances from my cell phone demanding
a race to the bathroom. No rest for the wicked,
as the saying goes.
I must be a wicked man indeed
to be woken while poems
still danced in my head. I will keep
my fingers crossed
that there is an email waiting for me
sent from you on your now
darkening side of this planet we call earth.

Hugs from Canada,
Tai
x

Zooming to You

November 27, 2020

Dear Basu,

Books are on the way to you from the UK,
much faster than shipping from USA.
I hope that you enjoy
the four or five that I sent.
With the wonders of Google Satellite
I zoom in on your rooftop.
Run outside and wave to me.
I see you are not very far from all of the trees
in the cemetery.
Not very far from the Subarnarekha River.
Not much traffic on Marine Dr.,
the riverside road.
Is there a nature trail along the river
for weekend walks with your kids?
Nice to see the top of your house,
maybe the top of your head.
One day we will meet in person.
Books will be dropping from the sky soon.

Hugs from Canada,
Tai

Covid Poems

Happy Spring 2020

Dear Bellyachers,

Saturday, March 21st,
an odd spring in world history
has arrived
with the world in self-isolation,
some in strict quarantine.
A mayor in Quebec is requesting
that their entire town be in quarantine.
Get outside
with your lover and loved ones.
Give them a hug in public if you want,
but maybe don't hug the public.

Let's put it all in perspective
and be grateful
that we are not living in quarantined times
of war where thousands and thousands
have died in atrocious conditions.
Oh dear, we have to self-quarantine,
oh dear. I can't get out
to McDonalds or Starbucks
and lounge in the neon glow
of being pampered.
Oh dear, I guess I will have to
self-quarantine at home
   and work at my computer
      and watch tv
         and have popcorn as a snack.
Oh dear.

Stay Safe,
Isolated Tai
xx

Before and After Time

May 10, 2020

Dear Brighton,

Mayor Brian Ostrander air fisted me
a hardy Poet Laureate congratulations,
six feet apart, in the yawning shade
of a stretching young maple
at the Brighton Municipal Offices.
A sunny day, masked strangers strolling
a "safe" distance from neighbours, smiling
with a warm reserve, no intimate contact
of hugs and kisses. We stood in the future shade
where generations will congregate
in the "After Times." The young will sit
on this polished stone bench, grey
and maybe contemplate
the social values that Brighton brought to them
from the long ago "Before Times" of 2020.
They might look back at the statistics
that we are right now creating, living, molding,
running from,
and not know what we had to endure
keeping our social separation, month after month
with family and friends in abeyance,
in what we now call lockdown –
I like to say cocooning.
They cannot possibly know that this sacrifice
is actually for them so they can sit
under this now young maple and enjoy
the maskless moment of sharing a hug with a friend.

Be safe, fellow Brightonites,
Richard Grove/Tai

Have a Wonderful Good Day

This is a poem that would not have been written six months ago.

July 18, 2020

Dear Brighton Friends,

Kim and I are well,
still cocooning in Presqu'ile Park.
Kim is so busy taking care of our B&B –
so many back to back customers this year.
People are aching to get out
of their own house into nature.
I am at my computer working –
supposed to be work working
but get sidetracked to write a poem
from time to time.

Going out means a mask these days,
so am staying in more than usual –
can you tell I hate the mask?
I would rather work at my computer
or in the garden and just wave to neighbours.

I had a masked clerk mumble something
at me the other day.
I mumbled back through my mask
with a polite nod,
my eyes did not smile,
past my steaming glasses,
mask puffing in and out,
the bellowed throat of a bullfrog.
Our heads nodded unknowingly
past the plexi covid panel
that kept us apart.
I mumbled a "have a good day"
and proceeded to put my groceries
back in the cart, to put them bagless

in the trunk – I forgot my bags again.
I almost forgot my mask.
At the end of the groceries
I found five folded bags. I think maybe,
in hindsight, the clerk
might have mumbled
"Do you want bags?"
I realized that she did not say,
"You are such an old hag."
I hope she did not think I said
"Have an awful day."
Or something worse.
As social beings we rely on our smile
to tell the truth.

So

Have an "awful" good day dear friends ,-)
You see, even in a poem
the smile says it all ,-)

All the best with your cocooning,
Tai

P.S. – remember to smile with your eyes!

The Last Sunset

January 1, 2021

Dear Family and Friends,

I went for a last walk
to our Presqu'ile Point Lighthouse
with Kim and dear friends
on the last evening of 2020.
The calm and tranquil time
of love and camaraderie
was greeted with a stunning sunset.
If we had headed to that
swell-swept grey-pebbled beach
a few minutes earlier, or later,
we might have missed the splendour.

That last sunset of 2020 was stupendous,
existing in a fearless, covid-free realm
of perfection. I imagined sharing
that moment with thousands,
maybe millions of equally stunned
blue-marble dwellers, all in awe with me.
I had to contemplate,
is there anything new under the sun,
except for our growing willingness
to plunge deeper with our faith
into a new pool of hope?

The restrictions imposed on us in 2020,
have of course, severely limited
our physical opportunities,
but as we closed out our walk,
in the covid-free zone of fresh air,
turning towards home, I thought
that there will be more

togetherness in the days to come, more
reasons to be grateful, more
blessed moments of now
for our faith in our fulfilled expectations.
As special as it was
on an ethereal, experiential level
to see that last sunset of 2020,
it will not be the last. The next sunset,
the fifth, the hundredth from now,
will be as cherished as this last of 2020.

The sun, the clouds, the waves,
the redness, the orange
will never be repeated in exactly this way,
but now that we have slipped into 2021
we are offered
a growing faith and trust in love
that our every need will be met
to our expressions of a joy-filled life.

Enjoy these covid lockdown days.

Hugs from Presqu'ile,
Tai
xx

Take the Time

November 30, 2020

Dear Poetry Lovers,

It is so easy for us to live
an insular life, tapping
out poems on our computers
in our private offices,
covid confined, or horizontal
in bed on our phones
blurry-eyed wishing
sleep would drag us
into the world of before.
What a wonderfully
comfortable risk-free world that is.
I am "almost" used to not leaving
my cocoon into the world
beyond my own self-creations,
but then I find in my inbox
an invitation that opens my world,
allowing me
the gentle joy of discovery
only a click away, transported
beyond a tree book
arriving in the mail, beyond
an eBook purchase, dropped
from the ether through
invisible wires into the blue glow
of your tablet.

Here I give you
the opportunity to travel
with me to India and bathe in the warmth
of generosity provided by
Jaydeep Sarangi and Basudhara Roy
and their invited poets.
Come and sink for a few minutes
into the rich bounty
of the poems they present.

I expect you will be as enriched
as I always am.

The Hearth Within Poetry Collages
https,//youtu.be/I5idLmGsPFw
https,//youtu.be/j1DN0Uqov7U
https,//youtu.be/sdiGmdqYRGw

Hugs from my covid-shrouded
monitor-flickering desk,

Tai
xx

Three Licorice Allsorts

April 3rd, 2020

Dear Brighton,

I am at my computer, working from home.
I am not bouncing off the walls
like some self-isolated
fellow brothers and sisters of this
growing smaller and smaller world
of pandemic isolation.

A trapped-bear friend of mine
needs to get out, he said, not so much
to see family and friends, to get a hug,
but to share fresh air with them,
stride the paths,
seek the horizon beyond four walls.

My self-isolation treat last night
while watching the eighth episode
of *Star Trek Picard*,
was recorded for me by Paul,
was to eat three – only three –
Licorice Allsorts. Three became
my treat for the evening. Three
is better than two, four
becomes the want of more,
more becomes a painful reminder
of isolation.

Your Poet Laureate,
Richard M. Grove/Tai

Letters Home from Cuba

Email Letter Home – 1

My Dear Kimber,

I am sorry but you will have to figure out
what you have read and what you have not.
Manuel keeps forgetting to send my email
for me and I am reluctant
to send from this email address.
I guess when you get this it will be Thursday.

I had an email for you every day.

I love you and will see you on Friday.
My flight leaves Holguin at 10:10am.
and arrives in Toronto at 15:00, Flight # 5031.
The ticket person at the Toronto airport
put the baggage stickers over my departure time,
so today with Martha's help I finally figured out
when I have to leave her casa.
I was thinking departing 15:00 = 3pm.
Oh man am I glad I double-checked.
I will be with you by 3:30 or 4 depending
on how slow my luggage is.

I hope there is something in this email below
that you have not read yet. Pass it on
to whomever you like *** after you fix my spelling ,-)

See you soon my dove.

xxxooo

Hola Mi Amor,

Here we are on April 2nd.
I am looking forward to your arrival.
I miss you every moment we are not together.

I will try to paste a message from my thumb drive
to this message on Manuel´s computer.
It is not all that complicated if
it were not for me being at a Spanish computer.

I just got back from climbing Cross Hill.
Almost 500 steps to the top carrying my bike
on my shoulder. The steps are organized
in sets of 25 with a small platform that usually
has a bench. I did 2 sets of 25 each time
before resting. 50 steps at a time got me to the top.
This grandi hombre is loco. 32°C.
Then I rode my bike down
the back side of the mountain into poverty.
I am sad to say that Holguin has such a slum.
I don´t mind seeing grass huts and cactus fences.
They just represent life of a different time
but I do hate to see
the stinking squalor that some people live in.
Slum is hardly the right word for how they live
on the back side of the mountain.
Their road that leads to their houses
is the road to the dump just past their houses,
a landfill area that is always smoldering.
Depending on the direction of the wind
the billow of stench drifts across the road
into every kitchen, into every backyard
where laundry hangs, into every open-air bedroom
into the street where half-naked children play.

I am at Ruben's computer.
With a little bit of imagination, pictures
and guessing what a Spanish word might be,
I have found the letter on my thumb drive
and am pasting it below.
I am supposed to be visiting with Wency a bit later
but it is still raining.
I hope it will stop so I can bike
down to him at the main square at 7:30pm.

I am here at Manuel´s for dinner again
so I should leave you now and
visit with them.
Say hi to everyone for me.

Hugs from Holguin.

xxxxoooo

Dear Kimber,

I hope you are saying hi to family and friends for me –
tell them that I don't miss them one little bit!!!!!!!!!   ,-)

I am having such a great but uneventful time.
Hours of writing in the mornings
and then some review / editing
in the evening before I go to bed.
For some reason I don't feel very inspired poetically
but I finished editing my collection of short stories
and today have written a 700-word preface for my book.

I went up to Cross Hill today. The word "hill"
is a bit of a misnomer. It is a MINI mountain.
First you have to walk, or in my case, bicycle
uphill to where the stairs start.
It is a workout just getting to that starting place.
Then you have to walk up 30 or 40 stairs
just to get to the platform where the stairs start
and then you have to walk up
the almost 500 stairs to the top. I have walked up
three or four times other years
but obviously it had been over a year.
I had forgotten just how steep and long the steps are.
I imagine that I am one of the very few
that have ever walked up
with a bicycle over their shoulder.
Yes, people were looking at me like I was loco.
Every 50 steps I stopped for a rest before moving on.

The view at the top is wonderful.
Cross Hill is at the top of a peak, so you can see
for many miles in every direction.
You can see the ocean on a clear day.
Kites, hawks, vultures, pigeons
all sailing the updrafts from the city.
As you can imagine, it is rather windy up there.
Do you remember that is the location
where I did the short series of paintings one year?

From the Top of Cross Hill

From the top of Cross Hill you look down
upon clouds' shadows cast
that roam the hills and flicker
a rusted rooftops glance.

From the top of Cross Hill you look down
upon the black backs of gliding vultures
balancing wind–swept that soar
in constant death-scoping vigil.

From the top of Cross Hill you look down
to poverty's bunkers dug
into earth's red crust where pride lives
in a new pair of Nikes traded for a smile.

From the top of Cross Hill you look down
to pigeon's gorgeous glide in
aerodynamic wing-whips
flying tip-to-tip formations of joy.

From the top of Cross Hill you look down
to the sprawl of people zigzagging
their way from one form of busyness
to another. The same busyness
that any city suffers.

* * *

What else did I get up to today?
I had dinner with Manuel and Adonay again.
They are so generous with their hospitality.
I saw some meat in a freezer in the store today
and almost bought some but I knew
they had little or no room in their fridge or freezer
so I resisted. I left their place early today
to meet up with Wency at 7:30pm.

I dashed off a little bit late
and met him in the main square.
We talked for a long time and then
he bought us both some ice cream
that we ate in the park. He is a generous guy.
I think that I am going to have dinner
at his home on Thursday night. I have invited him
to dinner at Manuel's on Wednesday.
Oh my goodness, I am starting to run out of days.
I wonder if I can extend my ticket –
just kidding. I miss you and will come home
on the prescribed ticket day.

And wouldn't you know it, Wency knows
my landlady Martha, from the university,
though he had not met Ruben before.
I met Martha and Ruben's daughter Keyla
and her husband, hmm …
I met him the other day and can't think of his name –
a very nice couple, friendly and easy to get along with.
They have a gorgeous baby girl – Kamila.
I met their son Maykel the other day also.
Such a very nice family.

* * *

I was cleaning up files from the laptop this morning
so I could make room to do a defrag
and came upon this file
that I sent you just over two years ago.

Friday March7, 2006

Today I packed up and left my casa particular at Deisy's and came to Gibara, a small seaport about a 35-minute taxi away – $18. CND

I had to stay in one casa particular and Manuel, Adonay and Pablo had to stay in another because they are Cuban. My political / cultural feathers are being ruffled, but I am staying quiet and safe – don't you worry.

Blue Cattle and Green Cattle

No, no señor, the blue cattle no stay with the green cattle at night. The blue cattle must sleep here and the green cattle must sleep there señor. Sí, sí señor, Tomorrow the green cattle and the blue cattle can get together and see each other again but they should never be together for certain things and never in the same pen overnight, señor. Next week some of the blue cattle will leave and some new blue cattle will come. No, no señor, the green cattle never leave, only the blue cattle can come and go. Sometimes we let the green cattle leave but only on a short leash. We learned that if we give them a long leash the leash might break and they will not find their way back. It is for their own protection, señor. They have everything they need here and nothing will hurt them. Sí, sí señor, they are happy here, we tell them that they are happy here and they don't want to leave if we keep the fence strong and high. We tell them that they love their home and they do. Only if a blue cow tempts them do they ever really want to leave.

Manuel liked my little metaphoric story. The metaphor is not soooo obscure. Do you think that anyone will get the point LOL. Like much of my writing on Cuba I am sure it will not get published.

Manuel was booked into a nice but low-grade casa particular, but because Adonay forgot her identification cards they would not let them stay. A green cattle without ID is no cattle at all. So here we were in Gibara for a holiday weekend and they had no place to stay. Well, Manuel talked the guy who organized their rooms for them into letting them stay at his house as a friend. Paying under the table. I have to tell you about that in person. This place used to be a registered casa particular but was so rundown that the Cuban government took away his license. Remind me to tell you about the squalor conditions. Manuel, Adonay and Pablo had to stay there and on top of that I had to hang out there with them because they were not allowed to come to my casa particular – no Cubans were allowed to visit. I think I am going to get tired of this green cow / blue cow stuff real quick.

We just got back from a walk to the ocean and the full moon was shining as big as a plate behind a palm tree. I wish you were here to see it.

I am in my casa with the a/c on getting ready for bed. We did go swimming today but I hope we will find a better beach so I can actually swim instead of paddle.

* * *

So that was part of my adventure two years ago.
Yesterday Wency came in to my casa particular
for a short visit. I don't know
if he was officially permitted
or if they were just tolerant
because Martha knew Wency from the university.
I remember that Deisy
two years ago used to make Wency register
if he stayed for more than 3 - 4 minutes.
Deisy was not happy to let me have visitors.
Manuel spent a few hours here with me
working one day. Again I don't know
if Martha was just tolerant
because Manuel is friends with her or
if the rules have become more relaxed.

* * *

I have commented on the patio garden here.
It makes the visit so pleasant.
I was asking Ruben about the name of a plant
that he has growing in a few places.
It is called – Malango de Jorden.
It has a beautiful purple green leaf.
In some ways the patio is not very special,
because on three sides it has a patchwork
of ancient bricks with
some not very careful concrete patches.
The floor of the garden
is rough patched concrete BUT the magic
of the place is the love and care that fills it.
Plants fill every corner in rusty old dinted pots.
Many varieties of plants are hanging on
or climbing up the six-foot wall.
It is a wonderful place to read, visit or work.
The birds are back; Ruben tossed some rice down.
There are three mourning doves,
a few sparrows and a few other birds
that I don't recognize that come and go.
The colour, a chalky light green,
is part of the magic of the place.
I do hope we can organize
a CCLA writers workshop here.

The Diaz Garden

In the Diaz garden
there is a magical plant
with purple-green
heart-shaped leaves.
Within days a piercing
purple spear emerged,
unfolded into a splendid
three-foot-tall leaf.

If you tried to pull at the leaf
before it was ready to open,
in time, in nature's time
you would only harm
the perfect leaf that would emerge.
I was thinking about this in relation to Cuba.
It needs to emerge slowly over time.
Just because Fidel has stepped down
it does not mean that the new leaders
should brutally tear at the country
and make it emerge
into its new stage prematurely.
The country will be torn apart
if reform happens too soon.
Fidel himself knows that change
has to happen. In his wisdom
he put his brother in charge
who has already made some small
growing changes that will grow
into the beautiful leaf that it should be.

Remind me to buy some picnic tablecloth clips
and give them to Martha the next time that I come.
They provide a wonderful large table
in the outdoor dining room for eating.
This is where I do much of my computer work,
but the tablecloths are forever flapping up.
These picnic table clips
will solve the problem for them.

See you soon my dove.
xxoo

Email Letter Home – 2

Letter home to Kim, Bill, Julie, Chris and Doug

March 28, 2008

Miamor, mi hermano y mi hermana,
My Love, My Brother and My Sister,

I miss you all, already.
I am in tears as I write;
tears of joy that I am here
with my long-missed family –
Manuel, Adonay and Pablo,
tears of gratitude that I am in a new amigo's casa –
Martha and Ruben are so loving and warm,
tears of sadness that I had to leave paradise
to be in *paraiso*, tears of sadness
because you are not here to share
this warm breeze with me.

Everything is perfecto, nothing –
absolutely nothing could be better.

I walked from the wings of steel to my –
unlocked luggage –
to find it untouched –
thank you divine Principle.
The lock of Love carried it off of the plane
to a waiting cab. My bicycle –
soon to be Manuel's –
is still packed in a slightly punctured box.
I will re-assemble it now and spin
my Canadian wheels over Cuban streets
to find my calm adventures.

My room with four louvered windows
looks out to the garden of content.
Through swaying green

I hear chickens clucking,
a neighbour's pig squealing
at scraps tossed. A dog,
barking at birds next door,
perks my attention from time to time.
This is the Holguin
that I have always known – children playing
in the streets, the clip clop
of horse-drawn carts moving people,
hay, plantain; moving everything
that needs to be moved.
Motorcycles zip past smoke-belching trucks
to meet destiny face-on with optimism.

I have to remind myself not to be fooled
by my false notions of prosperity.
Much is needed at Manuel and Adonay's
cave, as Manuel calls it,
concrete bunker, as I call it,
filled with love, filled with hope, brimming
with passion and warmth.
A new refrigerator stands with pride
on fate's expectation that – all needs will be met,
a new washer is poised to wash with pleasure.

Here is a poem that sprang to life in the millisecond
that I saw a beautiful lemon yellow butterfly
fly across the highway
on the way to Martha and Ruben's casa
from the airport.

See you soon.
xxooxxoo

Blown by the Breeze of Hope

for Martha and Ruben – March 28, 2008

Sweet lemon butterfly of protest
pierces pollution,
weaving past treacherous belching trucks
to safety of *paraiso*.

Royal palms sway, resolute
in political climate
of impending change.

The slight, ever-so-slight breeze
of looming capitalism, fanned
by hope's false promise
flaps Cuba's red white and blue.

Our beautiful lemon butterfly
perched suckling at the blossom
of now, the nectar of content.

     * * *

My room is wonderful, it has lots of light
and enters from the open-air dining room
which is basically two walls and a roof
that face the back garden. My room
has an air conditioner, a requirement of mine,
that pumps the cool breeze of guilt
for at least part of the night and a fan
that blows the rest of the time
over my unacclimatised, Canadian, pampered body.
My fear that you might have yet a last spring snowstorm
at our Brighton, almost an island, home
is at least consoled by the fact that you
could have come with me. Don't worry,
I am getting over the guilt of being here
and turning on the a/c. We will see if I have
the air conditioner on for more hours in nights to come.

Will my guilt of using electricity cave
to my need for pampered comfort,
or will my sense of entitlement cave
to my planet-saving conscience. As the new afternoon
heats to 28°C I can pretty much guarantee
how long my a/c will be on tonight.

How can I make this my winter home?
Martha and Ruben have a phone line,
I think also an internet connection. Hmm,
is it possible to run Hidden Brook Press
from the comfort of this paradise?
The wheels of imagination are turning.
How much will I have to pay every year
to make this the winter hub of HBP and the CCLA.
An internet connection may make my fantasy come true.
I will have to pick the right moment
to talk to Martha about the price for a long stay
with email.

I am learning about the ins and outs of Cuba.
I can now show you the Cuba that one will not see
if one spends one's time only on a resort-groomed beach.
You come for a week to a resort in Guardalavaca
and I will visit you there for a swim in the ocean
and then you can come and stay with me
at mi casa particular here in Holguin.
Hmm, the plan is unfolding.
Hmm, put it out to the universe and see
if it unfolds or folds in the shape of a kite or an envelope.
I may have a painted picture but the paint is still wet
and I am willing to have it be a different picture.
Whatever the picture, it will always be a beautiful one.

2:30pm – I have reassembled my bicycle
and have taken it for a spin.
I think I will have to tinker with the gears a bit,
but for now it is working fine. Brakes are tight –
no squeak, handlebars are true and
I have mixed some Cuban air
with the Canadian air in the tires.
Interesting metaphor – I will have to think about that.
I feel a poem coming on.
I will have to save that for later, as I told Manuel
that I would come to his place in the late afternoon.
I still have to buy some *agua con gas*
and a treat for Pablo, oh
and some juice for my dear sister Adonay –
she loves fruit juice.

See you soon, mi amor.
Kim I love you and miss you.
You should have come with me!!!!
Just kidding, mi amor.
I know you could not come with me.
Get your ORT book finished
and I will publish it when I get home.

Hugs.
xxxooo

Sunday March 30, 2008

I trust you are all well.
Yesterday I had a wonderful time
with my family, Manuel, Adonay and Pablo.
We sat and talked and talked and played
for many hours. The magic trick of
"make the string disappear" is universal.
I love playing with Pablo.
From one palm to the other
it could never be found. In the afternoon
Manuel and I went to the government store
to buy their food rations.
I was under the false impression
that Cubans received a free ration of some food items.
But this is not true. They purchase the items
including some soap and toothpaste
for far less than the regular market rate.
Their ration book that tells
how many people there are in the family
and their general age will prescribe how much food
they are allowed to buy. Everything is purchased
with Cuban (People's) Pesos (CUP)
not Cuban Convertible Pesos (CUC).
One CUC will purchase 25 People's Pesos.
One CUC will purchase one USA dollar.
This will give you an idea
of the value of the different pesos.

For the ration book everything is sold in People's Pasos.
For a family of 5 one will spend about 50 pesos (CUP)
for all of the rations for one month –
about 10 pesos per person.
A professional doctor or professor will be paid
about 30 pesos (CUP) a month. With the ration book,
rice is 24 centavos per pound,
sugar is 10 centavos per pound.
When you run out of rice
you will have to buy rice on the open market
for 10 times the price.

I was in the department store
buying my drink of choice –
agua con gas – $1.15 per 1 litre bottle (CUC).
I have found a cheaper place
that is on the way to Manuel's for $0.80.
I was also buying juice
for my juice-loving sister Adonay.

LOL I found an open chest freezer full of
upside-down ladies diving for meat.
You don't want to know the colour
of all of their panties.
From moment to moment
a friendly rummaging woman would surface
with a large frozen block of meat.
Looks of satisfaction whelm over all faces
with heavy rattling clangs that echo
to cart or wire basket.

As soon as I dared make my approach
this *grande hombre* was upside down,
bum sticking in the air.
Moments later, frozen fingers
like a deep sea diver. I return to the surface
with pride of frozen, sunken treasure.

Turning to a lady I ask,
"What type of meat is this, *por favor*"
"Si, si it is meat." she turns and disapears.
Another attempt – "*Lo sientosinoreta
mi Espanol es limitado,*
what kind of meat is this, *por favor?*"
The answer was a scowl
followed by a hasty retreat
into the anonymity of the bustling crowd.
Maybe she thought I was calling her
a hunk of meat – *Lo sientosinoreta.*

Upon presenting my frozen treasure to my hostess –
mi hermana – Adonay,
I discovered it was liver.
The largest hunk of liver that I had ever seen.
We will be having fried liver and onions soon for dinner.
I am not convinced that Manuel
is particularly delighted
with the prospect of eating so much liver. LOL

With the desire to feel safe
in their open-air concept homes, the occupants
often erect iron bars on their windows
and around their open-air dining and living rooms.
While this does make for a secure sense of harmony
in one's life it
also restricts movement between neighbours.
Here is a poem about the chain link fence.

The Phantom Hand

for Adanay and her forever smile

Water glugs
from bottle to pot
through floor to ceiling
chain link fence
smiles of gratitude are exchanged
for smiles of – you are welcome.

Beans are boiled in neighbours' agua.
Less salt or something the myth says
makes for better beans when boiled.

The phantom hand of camaraderie
appears in Adonay's kitchen from time to time.
Milk, cheese, slices of meat
pass in and out.
Joy of sharing a window between two kitchens
as its advantages.

While Martha is on email
I will see if I can send this from her computer.
I am on my way to Manuel's soon
so will finish writing later.

Hugs.
xxxooo

Email Letter Home – 3

My Dear Kimber,

My trip has mostly been calm and uneventful
though interesting and rewarding in many ways,
just what I need. Mornings and early afternoons
are spent at my *casa particular* working on my writing
with late afternoons and evenings at Manuel's.
I have gotten to know Pablo better again,
I have spent time with Adonay as a sister
and Manuel and I have spent much time
simply hanging out and editing some of his writing.

I hope to get to The Hill of the Cross sometime soon
and soak in some landscape inspiration
with my camera for paintings.

Tuesday April 1, 2008

Kim, you remember the tire hand-pump
that you dug up from the basement
so I could take it with me for my bike.
It worked for only a few strokes
and then it blew no air. Now I remember
that it did not work and had long been
designated for the landfill. Well the same genius
of need being the mother of invention
also translates as need being the mother of repair.
In true Cuban fashion I took it apart,
monkeyed with a flange on the inside,
put it back together, first the wrong way and then
the right way and it works fine.
It does not have enough power
to fill a tire all the way but I did ride
for a couple of days until I found
a gas station with an air pump.
Their air is still free here.
I am sure there is a poem in that idea.

Hi Doogla, mi hermano – I finished a final edit
of "Psycho Babble and the Consternations of Life."
I will give it to you for a final read.
It is wonderful to finally have time to finish it.
I think it is ready for publication.
I also wrote a preface that I hope you like.
I look forward to seeing it published by your imprint.
It is much better than the first ms.
I presented to you for editing.
I am planning trip up Cross Hill. I wish
you were coming with me.
There is a poem for you up there.

Manuel and I have been talking
about plans to bring a literary group to Holguin
and make it much more writing-oriented
than the Havana reading tour. I see ten of us
sitting here in Martha and Ruben's back garden
workshopping every morning during and after breakfast.
I see finished books coming out of the experience.

I love my long drawn-out breakfasts
in the open-air dining room that faces the back garden.
Birds of different varieties are hopping and chirping,
a rooster is still crowing off in the distance,
the pitcher of orgasmic orange juice perspiring,
the brimming plate of papaya ringed
by pale chunks of dripping pineapple,
a feast in its own right.
There is a mourning dove cooing its content.
Four buns, I eat two and save two for lunch
with my peanut butter.
Two eggs broken and fried flat
with a thick slice of fried ham.
I have learned to discreetly
dab the excess grease off
at the risk of offending my host.
Chunks of white cheese fill a saucer.
I eat it with the pineapple.

All of this food served with a pot of tea –
the tea that Kim so kindly reminded me to bring –
as the coffee, which I love, is not decaf –
they have not heard of such a thing –
has a deleterious effect on my body.
I am looking forward to a decaf Starbucks
as soon as I get home. Sarah, my darling daughter,
where are you when I need you?
Dare I import my own decaf next trip?

With my writing I manage to stretch my breakfast
well into the afternoon. Here I am at 12:40
and I still have a banana – oh so sweet –
and some orange juice. I do not have to stretch
my imagination to guess how
Hemingway must have lived. Palm fronds
bowing to the mango trees shading the ferns
and ferns that climb the brick wall
that is the home to those little lizard-type creatures,
are they called gingko, that dart
to their next motionless pose of safety.

* * *

Yesterday I took a ride on my bike
with the intention of circumnavigating the street
where I am staying. I keep having to first find
the city square with the church and the post office
and then find my way the four blocks from there.
Never have I managed to just come straight here.
Part of the difficulty is that the streets
are all one way here in this part of the city –
a common thing here that even the residential streets
are one way. Well, I went out and turned right.
Two blocks and turned right,
another two blocks and turned right,
another two and turned right.
Yes, eventually I got lost and had to find my way
down to the square with the church and come back

four blocks to find my home.
Last night I was determined not to overshoot my mark.
I turned confidently towards my *casa particular*
and found my way directly to the square with the church.
I am sure that the Cubans watching me,
LOL, must think that I am loco. Every street looks
so much the same,
low-rise pastel green or blue houses,
white painted grates on each window
sometimes ornate
often painted white.
Imagine yourself trying to find your way
in the thick of modern suburbia
where all of the houses, to you, look the same.
You turn the corner and find another palm tree,
another rusty stop sign,
another mango tree,
another giant split-leaf philodendron,
another dog that was maybe the same dog
but moved to another street.
Thank heavens for Cross Hill
and its radio tower lit.

Oh, very nice, a mourning dove
just flapped down from the stone wall
into the garden. I think that it is the same bird
that comes and stays at our place every summer.
Birds need no passports, they live without borders.
They do not recognise or care that I am Canadian
here or there. She struts her head, forever cooing at me
with no regard for how close
she has inadvertently landed.

How is your day, mi amigo? Are you going to
sit there all day and tap your fingers
or are you going to go out and see
what your day has to offer? My cooing friend
struts her head at me again and says –
If Kim were with you, you would be out there by now.

Well it is 1;20pm now and it is kind of hot,
so I think I will have a shower and a snooze —
just a short one to refresh and take
the long way around to Manuel's place.

I just talked to Wency, he called mi casa.
I am going to see him in the main square tonight —
Tuesday — he says hi.

I love you.
I am sending this to
Bill, Julie, Chris and Doug,
but give them a squeeze when you see them.

Hugs.
xxoo

11pm, A Cool Cuban Evening

January 2017

Dear Bill and Julie,

When are you coming to Cuba
with us again? With your jobs
we might have to wait until you retire.
Tonight there is a whisper of laughter,
chatter, from a group of five friends
under street lights, pale.
A pregnant woman, elegant,
standing in a long white dress,
content, rests her arm
on her extended belly, smiling.
This tranquil slow river of peace,
quiet, undisturbed by zipping
red Lada, belching into the dark.

See you in Canada soon,

Hugs.
xxooxx

To My Cuba Friends

At the Lake
for Jorge

May 4, 2008

Dear Jorge and Family,

what a great day it is.
kim and i just got back
from a bike ride
to the beach,
snoozed in the sun,
reading poetry,
up to my knees
in the lake,
too cold
for swimming.
mist rose
revealing sailboats
skimming
slicing distant deep fog
with piercing white,
gathered gentle breeze.
now back to the computer
to start layout of a book
then cover design.

hugs from Canada,
love you loads,
bro

Alligators Biting at Our Toes

September 13, 2021

Dear Jorge and Michelle,

Our summer is whispering to a close.
Kim and I were in swimming,
in Presqu'ile, lake side, the other day
as we very often do –
a three-minute bike ride out
our back door into the Provincial Park
to the calm grey slate pebble beach
that laps our northern shore. The water
was 20°C, the air was 22°C.
Just days before it was 23 and 23.
Our season of swimmable
is on the way out, though today,
in the Big Smoke, where I am today,
it was supposed to be
a high of 29°C .
We usually continue to swim
until we can't stand
the alligators biting at our toes
which is sometime
at the end of October.

I trust you are staying well and safe.

All the best,
Tai

Sometimes a Tomato

December 3, 2020

Dear Adis,

God loves you.
All of your human needs
are met by God.
Sometimes,
it is in the form of money.
Sometimes,
it is in the form of a laptop.
Sometimes
it is in the form of a tomato.
From me it is always
in the form of a smile
and my love.

Hugs to you and your family,
Tai

An Idyllic Moment of Now

For Manuel in Cuba

May 19, 2016

Dear Brother,

Right now, in this now of nows
it is a beautiful summer day
even though only mid-May
outside my office, high sun,
cloudless skies, birds chirping,
a smooth breeze – an idyllic moment.
Going to visit my daughter this afternoon.
In this idyllic moment of now,
not much could be better.

Bro

To and From
Canada and Cuba

A Hot One

July 13, 2016

Dear Miguel,

It's a hot one today.
The same in Cuba I presume.
Here it was 23°C at 9am. Climbed
to a promised brow-dripping 34°C.
A fire-breathing dragon chased me
to the lumberyard
to buy some wood for a shelf
that was on my honey-dew list,
a gentle nudge requested it be built,
soon, or was it now, I can't remember.
It took all day but am finally finished,
though one 2 x 2 short. Too hot
to drive and buy it.
This honey will do it tomorrow.
It was a two-beer – non-alcoholic – job,
I stopped to change my shirt
half way through the job.
Fan is on in my coolish
basement office.
Time for a snooze
in front of the computer
and pretend to work.

With affection,
Tai

Computer Broken

a found poem from Jorge

July 14, 2016

Dear Brother Tai,

Hello in Canada.
Sorry that my computer is broken now.
I can answer from Jose Pedro´s computer
now, everything is fine for the moment.
Finally I sold my boat and I bought
a new air conditioner in Bayamo yesterday
for my casa particular rooms
so my paying guests can sleep in cool.
My brother helped me to bring it to Gibara.
The bedroom is better now, for paying guests.

Have a nice night,
your brother Jorge

Routines – No Coffee

July 14, 2016

Dear Tai,

It´s a cold morning today, 20°C.
6:30am, my wife sleeps oblivious
of cold and noise and me.
I stretch my arms, feel my 50s already
but snatch myself out of bed
into routine.

Ran out of coffee the yesterday of a week ago,
no milk, must wrestle with the liquefier
to fix me a mango juice.
Bread and butter. Lucky!

I hit the stairs down with resolution
trying to erase some of my 50 years
cross the world
and plug myself into work –
a heap of papers and still another heap
with names and numbers dangling relentlessly.

The office computer crackles,
the screen spatters,
I caress the table with a thud and curse –
where the heck is the info I just typed?!

Lunch welcomes me,
three-course meal – rice, soup and pudding,
room-temperature drinking water
(the fountain broke today).

We resume our work,
can´t find the info yet,
spend two hours in this manoeuver
until the power switch-down saves me –
come back tomorrow, we´re economising.

Back home my wife says she is aching,
her arm hurts, can hardly move it.
Massage and Vaporub would do the trick
but I am already caught in the cooking ambush
survival mode.

A bit of after-dinner TV –
laughter stays with me until 11pm.
"Baby Daddy" is somehow twisted into Ancient Daddy.
My sleepy eyes blink and remind me I have a bed.

Tomorrow will be another day,
verbatim.

My hand,
Miguel the wingman

Raining

July 14, 2016

Dear Miguel,

A clap of thunder
shook the house last night at 2
in the morning. I was sound asleep
and leapt out of my skin. The rain
was so strong.
I did not know what the noise was
        – fire clawing at the house,
                a jet engine blasting
                        outside my bedroom window.
From my delirium
I discovered it was thunder.

I quickly fell back asleep and woke at 5am
to find the street was dry,
the air heavy and grey
clearing to blue in the afternoon.

I found a wet raccoon in the trap
that I had set the night before
I went to bed.
The family of bandits
has been ripping up my tomato plants
and attacking my bird feeders.
I will drive him to a forest where he can live
in peace with nature. My neighbour Brian
fed him a scrap for the ride.
I said I was going to drive my four-legged son
to camp. I hope he never comes home.

Today is an office day.
It looks like it might rain all day.
A good day for pushing words.

I hope Alina's arm is better.

Hugs from Canada,
Tai

First Gay Pride Flag
in the Neighbourhood

July 20, 2016

Dear Miguel,

Today I was installing
my new gay pride Canadian flag
that my gay daughter gave me
for Father's Day – at my request.
I don't expect any repercussions
from friends, neighbours
or our B&B customers
though you never know. One person,
within minutes of it being flown
called up to me on the front balcony
where it was installed and said
"what a pretty flag." Like my sister
she might not even know
that it is a gay pride flag.

Even though Brighton
is a bit of an anti-USA area
and just about everyone
that I have talked to says
they hope that Trump does not get in,
there is not really much of an anti-gay
sentiment here. We live in a bit
of a strange demographic.
A gay couple, women, no flag,
three houses to the right and
a gay couple, men, no flag,
to the left of us, though
there is a redneck across the street
that thinks all dogs, raccoons and gays

should be shot and a pro-USA neighbour,
otherwise a very nice guy, to the right,
that thinks that Canada
should join the USA as a state
even if Trump does get in.

The late Rob Ford, former Toronto mayor,
is the closest we have ever come,
to having a Trump-style state.
May he rest in peace with his
bombastic style. Some say
thank heavens he died in power.
God help the world if Trump
does become President of the USA.
Well anyway, I have my gay pride flag up
and it is the first in the neighbourhood.
Thank goodness for differences.
Gracias a bondad por las diferencias.

All the best,
Tai

No Break in the Heat

(Glen and Sonia Sorestad)

August 3, 2016

Dear Glen,

I trust all is well in Saskatoon
with you and Sonia.
I hope you have a/c,
at least in your bedroom.
I can only presume that it is hot there,
so says my android phone app.
Google Earth shows me you are just north
off of Yellowhead Hwy #16, not so far
from the river. Does the water level
in the South Saskatchewan River
ever get low? Our Lake Ontario
is starting to show some low water markers
that are usually under water
at this time of year. I am watering
plants this year that I have never had to water.
You can tell who in the neighbourhood
puts out the sprinkler every night.
They are the only ones that run a lawnmower
on Saturday morning. Everyone else
has a brown lawn that might need re-seeding.

Kim and I are well. Presqu'ile Provincial Park,
were we live, is 8 or 10°C cooler
than what the radio says downtown Toronto is.
The heat has not affected our B&B very much.
Last week we rented the entire house
to a wedding party. We went to visit
my 88-year-old mother, who is doing well.

Still publishing with HBP and now working
on my second novel, so all is well. A/c in my office
that looks out to clear blue skies
fluttered by my neighbour's Canadian flag.
If I crane my neck I can see water at a close beach.

Time to get back to work.

All the best,
Tai

Driving on the Edge

August 4, 2016

Dear Tai,

Your words speak of a severe heat, parching
that we have not experienced. Here,
where the temperatures have been more moderate
we are seeing what appear to be
bumper crops of every sort –
from canola to pulse crops to malt barley,
even the Saskatoon berry farms have produced
huge crops of heavy fruit. If all goes well
from here until harvest, there will be
many smiling farmers, once the fields
are harvested and the crops safely binned.
But we know, here on the great plains,
that a great many things can happen
before the harvest is complete
and any farmer will tell you
that most of these things are bad.
Including severe thunderstorms.

Sonia and I have just returned from Manitoba
where we found ourselves among members
of my mother's extended family for a reunion.
We greatly enjoyed the events over three days
and when it all wound down on Sunday
with a magnificent mid-morning brunch
we hit the road west from the little village of Argyle
to drive the seven and a half hours to Saskatoon.
As we neared the Saskatchewan border
we began to hear dire weather warnings.
Once we crossed the border
and rolled past Langenburg, the urgency
of the weather warnings ramped up
with tornado activity being spotted to the west
and south of Yorkton, so when we reached

that small city we made a hurried stop
to refuel our Pleasureway RV – the idea being
we were on the outer range of a huge storm
with severe winds, heavy rains
and even tornado possibilities –
none of which we found especially appealing.
As we sped west of Yorkton towards Wynyard
the near-black southern sky crackled with lightning,
the flashes against the dark sky
highlighted the dangerous clouds.
We drove through one torrential downpour,
so heavy that it all but scrubbed the vehicle
clean of all the accumulated Manitoba bug corpses,
an unexpected bonus of the heavy rain.
In our rearview mirror we could see
the blackened sky encompass the city
we had just fled and the next day we heard
Yorkton had been deluged by the rains,
while we made it home safe and dry.
We were fortunate in passing through Yorkton
when we did – had we arrived thirty minutes later
we would have been hit by the storm.
Sometimes it can be a good thing
to be on the edge of things.

May your novel work its way to fruition.
A novel is an undertaking for the intrepid
among writers and I cannot imagine the challenge
and the commitment required of the task,
so all I can do is to wish you well as you
journey your way through the fertile fields
of your imagination and your memories.

Our good wishes flow to both you and Kim,
along with the fond hope that the future
will allow our lives to intersect once more.

Warmest wishes,
Glen [Sorestad]

If you are ever

August 4, 2016

Dear Glen,

thanks Glen for your letter poem.
i have added it to my string.
i will keep you posted
if it ever gets published.

all the best to Sonia

if you are ever in our area
remember that our B&B rooms
are free to family and friends.

hugs from Presqu'ile,
Tai

Before Us on the Horizon

August 6, 2016

Dear Tai,

A special thanks
for the invite to be a gratis guest at your B&B,
should we happen to be coming to Ontario
during the coming months.
Your offer is greatly appreciated,
though it seems unlikely that we'll be availing ourselves
of your generous offer anytime soon –
no travel plans eastward
in the foreseeable future, though
as we are well aware,
we don't always have control over all the things
that lie before us on the horizon,
including where we may end up travelling.

We've had heavy showers the last few days
and today it's sunny, bright and warm again.
Our tomatoes on the back deck are ripening
in such an autumnal rush that we will be
hard-pressed to eat them fast enough
to keep ahead of the changing colours.
Such are the vicissitudes of life, I am told.
But life is good –
much better than the alternative.

Warmest wishes to you and Kim,
Glen [Sorestad]

Gasping Grass

August 6, 2016

Hi Glen,

Our rain today lasted for 2.5 minutes
and dried as it hit the gasping grass.
The humidity is almost unbearable.
Office a/c is pumping.

Hi and hugs to Sonia,
Tai

Love from the Family

August 5, 2016

Dearest Brother Tai,

I pray when you receive this, that your house is sold. It has become a nightmarish sale, brother. The most important thing, above all, is that you are healthy and happy, despite all odds. Canadian bureaucracy is, in some ways, the same as bureaucracy here in Cuba.

Summer here is hot, exceedingly hot, for our traditional summers. Many days are 35 and 37°C. Too hot to move when there is humidity. We did not have any rain in July, not a drop, but yesterday, God's blessing visited with some rain. Humidity and heat today tell of probably more rain, though we never know, for all summer has been humid and hot and with virtually no rain. Today, I came to the university on my bicycle, in the morning heat, to check email, and I have to leave before rain starts. I would rather have a hot shower at home with a bar of soap.

I am home all the time, studying, mostly, and enjoying my family and friends. Adonay is my sweet thing, now with some gray hair on her head, mellow and more lovely than ever. Pablo is almost as tall as I am. He will be as tall as you, Tai, tall like a tree.

I remember you every day, when I make coffee, when I cook something nice, when I buy mangoes, huge, sweet mangoes that drip from the chin. I wish we were neighbors, brother. We could go swimming in your ocean-size lake. By the way, I have to find some way to go there, maybe in the fall, if I found some way to pay for my trip with my work – I have a multiple entry visa until 2019. I will try to come for the CCLA Art and Lit Fest at the end of October.

Good for you with your writing, brother. I look forward to reading "Living in the Shadow." You are quickly becoming a novelist. The theme is very important. I suggest you mask the title of your new book behind a metaphor (you know better, of course).

I am attaching the call for *The Ambassador*. By the way, Adonay bought a new Nauta account for the cell phone. I will try it later, it is sad to be incommunicado, most of the time, in this world of Internet.

Love from the family,
Your brother, Manuel

A Fisherman Without a Boat

August 9, 2016

My Dear Brother Tai,

I went to the University in Gibara
and now I have time at the computer,
a rare commodity here in Cuba,
to send you a message.
We are fine at home, the children
are on vacation now,
Juampi with his pigeons and
Jose Pedro going to the park every night
with his girlfriend.
Michelle and I are working at home a lot,
for summer paying guests.
Finally I sold my dear boat to buy
an air conditioner for our paying casa guests.
The old one had no solution to be repaired.
I am really worriedly about that.
My boat, *Isabel Maria*, was part of my life.
But now she is gone, slipped from my fingers.
A fisherman without a boat is no fisherman.
We miss you a lot my brother.
I will go to my father-in-law tomorrow
because they have a new laptop
and I will have more opportunity to e-mail you.

Lots of love from your
Gibara family,
Kim, Tai, Michelle, Jorge, JP + JP

After the Hurricane

October 7, 2016

Hello my dear friends in Canada and Cuba!!!

This is an after-hurricane email.
You probably saw the news about Matthew,
the terrible storm that hit Cuba, especially
the eastern part, north of Holguín
and the south (Guantánamo and Santiago).
It was producing havoc in eastern Florida
and upwards yesterday.
It was horrible, Tai. I had to seal our
fifth-floor apartment the best way I could
and then climb down to the 3rd floor.
We were expecting wind gusts
of over 150 kilometers per hour.
I even had to board up the doors...
it was an awful experience. The night
in which the hurricane was supposed to hit Cuba
and devastate Holguín within hours
my diabetes numbers went up a little.
Fortunately not much, and I could control myself.
Hope all is fine up there with you. We are in
the recovery mode now, classes won't start
until Tuesday here in my university.
I came to check the mail and write to my friends.
The skies are serene now, the sun smiling,
pushing the clouds away. Lucky us.
Hope you get this one, some emails are bouncing back...
Give my love too to your wife and Danielle. She told me
she would be in Cuba for a while. Did she finally come???

My heart for you,
my friend,
Miguel the wingman

Nipple-Chilling Swim

October 8, 2016

Dear Wingman,

I went swimming yesterday.
The water was 16°C and the air was 13°C.
It was easy getting in
but nipple-chilling when getting out.
Though a gorgeous sunny day today.

Gotta run,
Tai

This Picture
To Freeze the Moment
for Posterity

Dear Jorge,

November 12, 2020

I am jealous, my dear Cuban brother,
that you are there with my Wingman, Miguel
in an embrace of brotherly love without me
(where are your covid masks)
celebrating your 59th birthday, with
two fingers of Havana Club rum,
a plate of banana chips fried with love
by my dear sister Michele, and what are those
other Cuban-looking things
that look like fried Polish perogies?
Save me one. Save me a finger of rum,
just one,
and make me fresh banana chips
when I come for a visit in the winter
if corona restrictions allow me to travel.

From the distance of too many miles
I send my love dear brother,
Tai

wishing

July 16, 2009

Dear Jorge,

as usual i am in a rush
so must not spend
too much time
at this keyboard with you.
no time to tap fingers
to chattering keys
with you other than to say
i longingly peer
through slatted
bamboo office blinds
to breeze-fluttered
red and white,
painted on cloudless blue.
my lake is calling me,
i can see it from my desk
if I crane my neck,
but i resist.
i stay anchored to my desk,
kayak dry,
upturned,
yellowing, shadowed grass
beneath. I am drawn
back to the glow of monitor,
task at hand,
wishing
I had my feet
under your table.

Tai

Gracias

January 2017

Dear Katherine and Enrique,

Gracias Katherine y Enrique
Gracias Cuba
For bringing us fourteen together
to spill poetry
into the Cuban air from your balcony,
proud, under the silver sliver moon.
Jupiter, descending in the west,
a bright beacon sinking
into the ocean that splashes
our mutual shores of friendship.

Looking forward
to the next Holguin CCLA reading.

Hugs,
Tai

A Conversation
Looking in the Mirror

Owed to Martin Durkin
Something he said in one of his poems sparked this one.

September 10, 2019

Dear Wingman, Miguel,

Thank you for all that you do
for HBP and the CCLA. Without you
we would flounder but not sink.

These lines came to me when
reading a book of poetry by Martin Durkin.
I would not tweak you even one little bit.

Just how much would you like to fine tune me?
Tweak my sense of humour, my creativity,
my earnest sensibilities of work ethic?
Just how often would you send the blueprints
for me back to the maker to be tweaked?
A little taller, shorter, fatter, thinner,
a bigger, smaller bridge on my nose.
Well, too bad. They broke the mold.
You are stuck with me just the way I am.

You are stuck with me and I am
stuck with you just the way we are.
Perfecto, gracias.

Tai

NOT
For Miguel

Dear Wingman,

January 28, 2021

On this
blue, sky-filled day
turning to clouds,
-8°C
I see an email from you
flash
across the bottom
of my computer screen
reminding me
that I am not
sitting with you
with a Jorge
special coffee
at fingertips
sipping
the aroma of Cuba
with our feet
under
our dear friend's table.
My windowless office
is filled
with the blue glow
of dancing pixels
that spell work,
work and
more work.

In these
covid-restrained times,
government lockdown
with no
international travel in sight,
it saddens my lament
that it might be
very many months
before I can
put a poetry book
in your friendly hand.

As my saying goes,
in a rush,
gotta go.

All the best,
Tai

Spring

Owed to T. S. Eliot
and the first stanza of his poem
"The Waste Land"

April 5, 2019

Dear Miguel,

You should feel lucky
that you live in Cuba. For us
in Ontario, April
can be the cruelest month,
with temperatures rising
finally into life, even at night.
Lilac buds are kissing
the warm air with swelling sprouts
stunted by the still,
frost-threatened landscape
that swirls memory with desire
only to be slammed
by her sister, winter's
punishing joke.
With the last of shadowed snow
the melancholy reminders
of hunkering down
are all but gone.
Black budding branches bulge
with the promise of life
now full of winged music
singing to pale-faced
sun worshippers praying
that it will not snow – again.

I hope to see you on a beach
in Cuba sometime soon.

Tai

The Side Effect Is Happiness

Half owed to Ralph Waldo Emerson
for Miguel my wingman

April 7, 2018

Dear Wingman,

Ralph Waldo Emerson
at least got it mostly right.
The real purpose of life is to be useful,
to be honourable,
to be compassionate.
This will make a positive difference
to humanity in general
and to the lives of individuals specifically.
What Emerson forgot to add was
the side effect of this noble lifestyle
is
that it will make you happy.

So basically be useful and honourable
as you are with me and you will be happy.
Say hi to Jorge
our useful and honourable amigo.

All the best,
Tai

Turning Fifteen
with a Rented Moment

Dear Miguel,

Very nice pics of your princess daughter.
She must be very pleased with her parents
for hiring an expensive photographer
to make her beauty immortal
though I have to admit that I think of it as
a very strange custom to put on rented clothes
to sit in a rented car
with a rented face
with a rented pose from a glamour magazine
so the girl can feel like a woman
for a rented moment.
Does any fifteen-year-old girl have a clue
as to what a catastrophic hit to the budget
it was and how many meals
it cost for the extravaganza?
To stage the make-believe.
The world of make-believe.
The princess has grown up playing with dolls
and now is the princess the doll
even if only in make-believe?

All for tradition,
Tai

Happy Birthday Pablo

June 2, 2010

My Dear Godson,

I can still see you playing on the beach
at Guardalavaca playa with Joshua,
your young Canadian friend.
Prosperity frolicking with poverty,
the Prince and the Pauper comes to mind.
For that moment you and he were both princes,
swimming in the innocence
of every wish fulfilled.
You and he in your slim boyhood, waves
tossing you both like waterlogged driftwood
pulling your feet from under you
bobbing in limbo captured by forces
neither pushed to freedom nor tugged back,
landing on the soft sands of content.
No politics here, at least not for you or him
for now. One day you may feel trapped
in paradise by the endless push and pull.
One day you will seek the undertow,
face its dangers that will drag you
to what you may wish to call freedom.

Hugs,
Uncle Tai

Quite a Handsome Bug

June 11, 2013

Dear Pablo,

I stopped and looked at a bug today.
He visited me while I was working.
It is a very fine thing to work hard,
being busy instead of idle.
Being creative, making, producing
are all gallant pursuits, but when a bug
comes for a visit and says "Hey,
what are you doing up there?"
it is time to stop and pay attention.

He was quite a handsome bug,
no longer than the nail on the middle
toe of a nine-year-old's left foot.
He had an orange and black body
with jet black legs and a head so shiny
that I can only imagine it was also black.
His eyes were rather larger than yours
or mine if we had been that small.

Where he came from I don't know,
but he was crawling on my desk
right in front of me. I can type quite well
without looking at my fingers,
so how long he was there I just don't know,
but when I looked down there he was,
crawling from Q to W,
looking up at me saying hello.
"Hello there, big man," in a squeaky voice.
"What are you doing tapping on that board?"

I gently put my finger down for him
to crawl up on, which he did
with remarkable eagerness.
I asked him how he was.
He bowed politely, wiggled
his black antennas at me and said
in a not-so-alarming voice
that he was fine.

From my finger I put him on my hand
so I could reach for my magnifying glass,
which any sensible person
should always have at his desk
for just such an occasion.
I peered down on him
with an inquisitive mind,
examining him from tip to toe
for a couple of minutes
before I said to him that I really must
get back to work.
With a puff I blew him from the hairs
on the back of my arm.
He flew away with a buzz,
landing on the windowsill a few feet away.

Where he is now I don't know,
but I am sure he is happily
doing bug-type things,
crawling, sniffing, exploring. I am sure
he is quite happy, maybe even telling
his friends, like I am you,
about our visit.

Say hi to a bug at least once a day.

I love you,
Hugs from Uncle Tai

A New Day Dawning
in the Quietude of Anticipation

March 10, 2021

Dear Pablo,

Here is a poem inspired
by one of your photographs
that you took in China.
What a wonderful pic!
You have a wonderful eye.

In the early hours of yesterday,
the hush of quiet
filled the dewcovered streets
with the yawn of inactivity.
A new day is dawning.
The fruit vendor, Lao Lin,
with drowsy anticipation,
tenderly places his fruit,
the sweet smell of citrus,
a rainbow of orange,
on display for when
the city of Guangzhou
will finally come to life.

All is still quiet, no honking,
no hustle bustle of pedestrians
zigzagging through weaving cars,
no screaming sirens
shrieking over vendors'
beckoning chants.

For now
in the quietude of anticipation
all is calm.

With hugs and thanks,
Your Godfather,
Tai
x

a desk glance at a full moon

October 23, 2010

Dear Manuel,

oh my goodness
i just looked up
over my computer monitor,
past the spent orchid
potted on my sill,
past the compact-fluorescent glare
on windowsill,
past the black
silver-traced cedar
across the street,
past the lamp post,
past the shifting clouds,
to the beam-hovering glow
of a full moon.
it reminds me
of just how huge the sun must be
for there to be a full moon
and no eclipse,
how small i am.
but still my thumb
extinguishes its glory.
i move my thumb
and the clouds have shifted,
obliterated its existence.
the moon had gone.
now only a fractured
moment later it is back.
how fast is it travelling
while standing still for me?

hugs dear brother,
Tai

Right for a Change

December 15, 2019

Dear Brother Manuel,

All is well here in Canada.
Kim and I are at the condo in Toronto.
The weather prediction was too dire –
rain that could easily turn to ice –
so we didn't bother going
to Presqu'ile for the weekend.
As it turns out, the weather man
was right for a change. The storm
predictions were correct.
Presqu'ile is beautiful even in a storm,
but driving two hours in heavy rain
and ice did not appeal to me.

Here is a short poem that I wrote.

Tai

After the Storm

Black branches dance
at my midnight window
in grey peach haze,
a leafless maze,
a bobbing zigzag labyrinth
leading nowhere beyond
the melancholy whisper,
    a gentle moan,
        a calmed reminder
of today's beast called winter.

Now after the storm,
a growl stilled
to purr of sanity.

I trust you are well and still
enjoying your teaching in China. Stay busy.
It will keep your mind off of Cuba
and your darling wife, my dear sister Adonay.

Hugs from Kim and me.

Bro

Blue Jays and a Distant Crow

For Manuel

December 12, 2017

Dear Brother,

Some months before I was sixty-five
I was walking alone,
along the north shore of Lake Ontario,
where you have stood with me
shoulder to shoulder gazing
at the immensity of my ocean-size lake,
facing south over my fresh-water sea.
Cuba and José Martí were on my mind,
reminding me of the delicate balance
of knowing the infinity of now,
this sacred moment, the silent chill of winter
crawling over the landscape
wrapped in shorter days.
The equinox of darkness hung in the trees, empty
abandoned nests clinging to naked branches of grey,
time's reminder that spring is painful months away.

The cheeky taunts of Blue Jays catch my attention
and the haunting caw of a solitary distant crow
are my only company echoing over the pasture
of frost-covered grass,   silver.

I wish you were here with me.

Hugs from Canada,
Bro

Owed to 'Yellow-Throated Vireo"
by James Deahl, page 26 of Red Haws To Light the Field

Hidden Among the Rocks

December 30, 2019

Dear Manuel,

Here we are
at the end of December.
Only small patches of snow
remain hidden
among the rocks.
Tomorrow it will be
well above zero again.
Jacket temperature for sure.
No snowmen
or skating memories
will be made
in Southern Ontario
this holiday.

I hope that I see you in Cuba
and your steel-winged trip home
from China goes well.
I will give and get a hug then.

Hugs from this side of the planet,
Bro
x

*This line is from Kate Rogers' FaceBook Post on December 26, 2019 —
Only small patches of snow remain among the rocks.*

No Cabin Fever

For Manuel in Cuba

Jan. 24, 2016

Dear Brother,

No cabin fever for Kim and me.
We just got back
from a 90-minute snow-filled hike
through the still calm woods
to the lake. We sat
on the banks of chattering ice
mesmerized by a rose horizon
melting
into the grey ice sheets
moaning
in the distant,
mist-filled forever.

Wish you were here,
Bro

Life in Toronto

April 21, 2018

Dear Brother Manuel,

Life has had me in a spin for the last few months.
Buying the condo was a wonderful thing for us
but I have not yet quite fitted it into my life
without it creating complications. My full HBP office
is still in Presqu'ile. I have a good laptop and now
a super-duper computer at the condo,
a necessity of life.
I just bought a second side-by-side monitor
so my condo office is slowly mimicking
my Presqu'ile neck-craning lake-view office.
I still have to load a lot of software
to be fully up and running.
It is a slow and sometimes painful process.

BUT, for me, living at the condo is linked
to a new part-time job as Maintenance Manager
for our dear downtown Toronto church.
This is very much a 'serve-the-church' job. While I am
happy to receive the modest part-time paycheque,
it does cause my life to spin in a different direction
than it did when we lived exclusively in Presqu'ile.
Working for the church demands at least
40 to 50 hours per month from me.
Between driving time to and from
Presqu'ile to the condo
and to and from the church it stacks up
to be an added 20-30 hours of travel time in a month.
I am not used to having 60 to 80 hours ripped
from my HBP, CCLA, writing life that I luxuriated
in while basking in the glory of Presqu'ile,
our Provincial Park haven.

If it had not been for my push
for us to buy the condo for Kim
because her family is in Toronto
and she is the church manager
for our Toronto church,
then I would not have even considered
the whiplashing shift
in lifestyle but Kim is so happy
that we bought the condo,
this makes me happy.
As the saying goes,
Happy Wife, Happy Life.
I so truly want what makes her happy.

There are lots of wonderful things
that are linked to the condo
but I am still very much in a state of adjustment.

When China permits,
maybe you can come to Toronto to visit.

With love and affection,
Bro
x

thick silver haze

For Manuel in Cuba

May 31, 2011

My Dear Brother,

i took a short, calm
bike ride to lake's edge
today. she was still and grey
motionless
covered
with a thick silver haze that glowed
in the cloudless afternoon.
the air was warm
hot in the sun only chilly in the water.
i took the plunge.
after a tiptoe entry
i stood waist-deep splashed
surface warmed water
on my chest and dove.
first swim of the season
late this year.

i thought of you as I finned
across slate-pebbled bottom
through milky cold depths plunging
to the surface for air
invigorated.
another dive
deeper
further out meeting mist
swallowed by timeless grey
wishing that when I turned around
i would see palm trees and the belch
of a 56 Ford then
back on my bicycle to put my feet
under your table.

hugs from Canada,
Bro

Out-stretched Branches, Grey

For Manuel

January 20, 2019

Dear Brother,

My mind wandered this morning,
thinking of you today
as Kim and I drove to work at our church.
I had to meet a contractor there,
the boiler guys,
to talk about the prices
for a major overhaul
sometime in the future.
This part-time job as maintenance manager
keeps me a bit too busy.

I was thinking about your trip
to Ontario from Cuba
and that we did not spend much time
in Toronto. We will have to do that
one day, now that we have our condo.

On our way to work
we drove through the quietude
of a barren January,
a birdless cemetery
on Rosedale Valley Road,
a tunnel of tranquility,
a corridor to and from Toronto chaos
where bones dissolve,
from the past into the future, draped
by strewn, brittle
outstretched arms of death
sliding, slow-motion

clinging to life, once extended
to timeless blue skies
now fallen into the oblivion
of the cycle of life
melting into starving frozen earth,
grey, feeding the next generation.

Hugs from the condo,
Bro
X

Soon

for Manuel

September 20, 2011

my dear brother,

once a month the silver-orbed rabbit
on his bicycle
peers through drifting eastbound
10pm grey into
my office window
on this 2011 tuesday
of mid-september.
the month and time drifts
with the clouds across brilliant moon
bringing the inevitable chill
that thrusts my pang for cuba
that will bring me soon to your table.
the canada geese honk and V
south calling me to follow.
i have plenty of work to keep me busy
until mid-december but then
an iron wing will tear me
from kim's embrace
where with torn heart
i will long for her and my canada
though soothed
by your fresh market piña
placed beside my darling sister's
rice and black beans
that only she can make
with such love.

see you soon,
bro

sun is shining

January 6, 2010

Dear Brother Manuel,

Buenos días mi amigo.
almost afternoon,
sun is shining,
not too cold,
clouds are drifting,
trees are still,
animal footprints
in new-laid snow,
birds
are joyfully gathering
in flailing flocks

All is well

Hugs from Canada
Always thinking of you

Brother Tai

This Place Called Now

a letter poem from one brother to another
Manuel and Tai

February 2009

Estimado Hermano / Dear Brother,

Beautiful here mi hermano, sunny and fresh, a little windy,
the fields, they are filled
by the colourful little flowers
of late Cuban winter.
This morning your sister, singing in happiness.

Good afternoon, my brother.
I see you were online at the moment I was getting email.
This is the closest that I feel to you when our electrons
cross paths and our email syntax fills the ether.
Thank heaven for the miracles of melted silicon and wires.
At this moment, in my place of winter, at my desk
        I am looking out to a breathtaking half moon painted
on a rippleless blue canvas. Such a gorgeous day.
I know you are looking at the same moon.
The sun and the moon bring our desks closer, my friend.
        They bring us to this place called now.

I got your email today. Such a busy man you are
with so many things to do in your life.
You will live to be 110 because you will forget
to stop and die. I miss you and Cuba, mi hermano
        the coffee, the rooster's crow
        the snorting pig from beyond.
        I miss the red earth – *la tierra roja*
        the foundation for where you sink your roots.

Today is only moderately cold -17°C
but the sun, the same sun that warms you
is filling my Presqu'ile home, bringing me
a little taste of Cuba spread across
my livingroom floor,
honey spilled from the pot of longing.

I wish, I so very much wish, I could be with you,
my sister Adonay, and Pablo for dinner tonight,
put my feet under your table
and join in our family time.

Hugs from beyond this time of place.

For place is now, forever here,
now this cool air over my island brings
aromas of your pine groves.
The earth whirls east and I see
the frozen breath of my tall brother,
in heavy coat walking by his lake.

Now is a place to meet with Pablo
in need for tales to go to bed,
his heavy eyes, his tiny voice,
his rough nobility of innocence.
The earth will whirl, the wind will blow,
the child he is now forever gone.

Love is timeless and is its own place;
hermano mío, your now is here
forever here.

Bro

Traditions

July 27, 2014

Dear Manuel and Jorge,

I wish you were here
to see the construction.
It is coming along very well.
The roof is almost off,
ready for the wall framing.
The Canadian tradition,
I am sure you have something similar
in Cuba,
is that men get together and talk
about tools, construction and materials
and admire the work that has been done.
Oh, and we also talk about women,
sometimes our wives,
and how wonderful they are –
yes they truly are, for putting up with us.
We do all of this with a beer in hand –
though mine with no alcohol
while smoke billows from the bbq
where fat burgers with dripping bbq sauce
simmer dripping to hot burners.
It all sounds very sexist but the women
are in the kitchen talking about
what a good job we men did
on the construction project while they
make potato salad.
As it turns out, I guess both sides are sexist,
loving how simple life can be.

I wish you were here,
LOL; with your wives
helping with the dishes.

Bro

The Onset of 2021

December 31, 2020

My Dear Brothers and Sisters and God Son,
(Manuel, Adonay, Pablo, John and Cathy)

Happy New Year from Kim and me.
Here we are, all trapped by geography
on different latitudes and longitudes
wishing we could all be together
with our feet under the same table.

Some on our big blue marble
have already greeted 2021
with confident enthusiasm.
Manuel and Pablo in China
12 hours ahead of us have already
tipped a glass of cheer.

Hours ago Aukland and Australia
have already fearlessly gathered
by the thousands
for an unbridled celebration,
unmasked, swarming the streets
unabashedly hugging
as if covid did not ever exist.

A friend just reported to me that India,
with numbers way way down
from the spike of mid-September,
has no lockdown as such.
LOL, my friend said,
"India seems to have forgotten
covid ever existed.
They have opened schools
now for grades 10 and 12.

Malls are all open.
Weddings, trains, journeys,
are all flooded with people.
Masks are still mandatory
but then there are plenty of idiots
among us in our country
where we can hardly force people
to wear helmets in their own interest,
so it is obvious you will find them unmasked."

Kim and I just got home
from a walk with Julie and Rosie,
no hugs and mostly 6-foot distance
albeit four-footed Rosie, leashed,
no mask, was all over me hugs and kisses.
Lots of people are out for walks,
in the woods, along the lake —
no covid lurking,
hanging from the trees there.

Our neighbour brings her girlfriends
and their dogs into her back yard
for a covid-free romp, no indoor tea
for them or for us but dear Julie brought
us a wonderful looking dessert
because we will not be able to have
an indoor visit with them,
though another walk is in order.

Friends in Gibara, Cuba,
brother and sister Jorge and Michelle,
say that family are mostly mask-free now.
Dinner with their priest
will bring in the new year

with a covid prayer of safety for all.
By the way, I heard he has covid now.
Their friends are gathering
for a roasted pig.
Let's hope everyone stays outdoors
and stays safe.

Have a great 2021, dear friends and family,
but remember that this covid thing
is not over at the stroke of midnight
though we hope to see you in person
months down the road for a hug.

Air Hugs and toe taps to you All.

Kim and Tai
xxoo

Thank You Canada

July 1, 2020

Dear Canada,

I have walked both of your salt-sprayed shores
east and west and every province between.
I have slipped my kayak
into your still-morning lakes,
mist-covered quietude, north and south.
I have shared wild blueberries with black bears
on a crisp September morning in Newfoundland,
berries baked into smoke-billowed pancakes.
I have hiked and climbed
your cloud-raked Rocky Mountains
in Banff and Jasper and sailed
into the sea-tossed Straits
off Vancouver shores.
I have hiked into the wilderness
from Terrace, BC and found
the eye of Canada, a small glacier-fed lake,
an oasis surrounded by ancient
moss-covered logs.
I have pitched a tent
on the shores of Saint Pierre and Miquelon,
gazing longingly east
to Canadian rocky shores.
I have rafted the Bow River
in calm and turbid waters
and cross-country skied
from Banff to Canmore simply to see
the Hoodoos covered in fresh snow.

Now in my late-summer years,
Canada has become the friends
I meet on the quiet streets of Brighton,
or as I walk out from my back yard
into Presqu'ile Provincial Park.
Now in these 2020 lockdown days
of social distancing,
I have the pleasure of leaning on the fence
jawing with kind neighbours
talking about the Barred Owl
I saw perched on my back deck
or the fox family that lives across the street
in the boulder cliff that looks north
to the ever-present Osprey-nested lighthouse.
For me, Canada is the three-minute chitchat
that I have in the middle of the street
with birdwatchers that return
year after year to drink in the beauty
of pine-swept skies of our Canada
that I never take for granted.

Thank you Canada,
Tai

The Wish of Shoulder to Shoulder

Dear Julie,

Kim and I wished we had been in Presqu'ile
with you waiting for the eclipse to happen.
Feet up on your deck gazing
at the darkening clouds with you.
Sorry Bill is in China,
would have made the eclipse day more special.

For us in Toronto,
on these few square metres of terra firma
the eclipse was, shall I put it bluntly,
a boring, dull grey, a dud of an experience.
Not even the birds went to sleep.
Squirrels still scampered up our tree peering
into our fourth floor as they stopped to nibble
on the new yellow spring shoots
of our Maple tree. Even though you had full clouds
at least you had an eerie orange horizon,
thanks for the pics.

Here is a poem that I just wrote.

Hugs from the Condo,
Tai

Moving into Totality,
A Cosmological Experience

Thanks Julie for your email that I stole
from and massaged into this poem
3:21pm on April 8th, 2024

It was a moving experience
even though it was cloudy.
We could not actually see the eclipse,
but we felt a deep hungering,
a longing for a cosmological connection
rooted in the thought-provoking desire
to be connected with divine Law.

We stood still in the absence of time
and considered our true
profound connections to the divine.
Moving into full darkness
there was a rim of orange
where the water meets the sky,
where the divine
meets human consciousness.
It was exhilarating.

As the sun and the moon
moved into totality,
the astrophysical laws
of the universe spoke to me saying,
At this moment,
at this millisecond,
at this place,
we are all the witnesses of
divine Law in action
and we will all be connected
from this moment on
simply because we, together, witnessed
the cosmological laws
of the universe in action.

I imagined
how people must have felt
before the solar system was understood,
the sun revolving around the flat earth.
Sister moon in a different orbit
putting the earth to sleep.
Understanding or not, does not change
the divine Laws of the universe.
Thousands and thousands of years ago
birds stopped singing and it got colder
just as it did today.
Then just three minutes later,
the light returned as divine Law demands.
The dawn chorus started,
birds woke into singing
knowing nothing of time.
We walked down the beach
where there were no others,
just a lone blue boat tethered
bobbing on the water obeying
the laws of adhesion, cohesion and attraction
the same way the moon, the sun and the earth
are always doing.
It was as if we were alone in the universe
joyously governed by divine Law.

Afterword from the Author

As I close the pages on this ms. I have to finish by giving ample thanks to Miguel Ángel Olivé Iglesias, otherwise known to me as my "Wingman" – he calls me the "Pilot." He and I correspond between Canada and Cuba by email and WhatsApp between 3 and 30 times in a week. We are brothers, poetry brothers, editing brothers, publishing brothers and philosophy brothers on many levels.

We are so often talking about time in one way or another; I am going to bed at 2 or 3am, as a night owl, as he is getting up at 5 or 6am; the electricity is most often out in his Cuban city of Holguin for 6 or 30 hours; I will request a fast turnaround on a piece of writing that he is doing for me; or I will say No Hurry, No Worry. Time filters into our lives in so many ways.

One day after a banter back and forth – that week it was more like 50 emails – I sent him this philosophical line. I will not try to explain the context of why I wrote it but I said, "Sorry my imagination thought the water picture looked like a river. A river that flows from the past into the future with the splashing waves of now." Miguel's quick reply was, "For a Zen Buddhist it is just the same."

From that email back and forth I wrote this poem and dedicate it to him:

a river that flows

to Miguel Ángel Olivé Iglesias

in the dance of timeless existence,
a river of moments cascades, flowing
from the past into the present
into the future with splashing ripples of now.
each sparkling droplet of time, fragments
of memories, hopes and dreams, undulate
through time's seeming fabric of
past, present and future. along its banks,
echoes mingle with dreams and hopes,
yet to be realized.
through the valleys of inevitable growth,
time meanders, carrying stories etched
in sand only to be washed away
by the next epiphany. every eddy and whirlpool
holds secrets untold, waiting to be discovered
by fearlessly navigating the present.
in now's gentle embrace, we find
relief in hope's promises of tomorrow.

Afterword by Miguel Ángel Olivé Iglesias

Short Lines That Made a Poet

I can proudly state I have read most of Richard M. Grove's literary work. I can also say I have at home many of his books, either print copies or PDFs. In reading him, I have come to know a man of depth and breadth. Grove is a DNA poet whose dedication to literature and art in general has opened wide for him the doors to what I have termed the PoetDom [Poets' Kingdom].

This letter poems book I write about reveals for us the intimacy and warmth of a man who sees beyond everydayness and what may seem just routine to the outside eye. Grove holds a magic wand in his hand and turns the facts of living-socializing and his personal connections with family and friends into chronicles of endearment and documents of contextual value. The poet succeeds, because he has the sentience and the insightfulness to do so, in registering for posterity the profound links he has forged along his life.

The book allows us to feel closeness, sincerity, appreciation, understanding, compassion. It leads us through a sea of sentiments that flow as the lines flow. No matter whether the letter poems are addressed to his beloved wife, his parents, his family, his friends, a higher constant will always greet us on every page, love. Grove speaks with the heart as he writes with the mind. Both blend harmoniously and give birth to unique pieces which, however apart temporally and spatially, simply originate in and receive greater truth from a man whose sensitivity transpires across the book.

As the poet tells in one of his letter poems, let us "contemplate the meaning of life" as we journey along the wondrous path Grove has paved for us with these moving samples of friendship in any form, of love in every sense. Because his lines, generally brief but packed with caring and humanity, are about human relations in their rich hues and manifestations. Grove's lines won't go unnoticed, every reader will strongly, inevitably relate to them.

The letter poems in this fine book will hold out and linger, as they are little gems that tell us of a man's own world, but they will also echo in the readers as they will see themselves reflected therein. In sparking such a bond, this book becomes indelible. Every reader, regardless of age, gender or literary preference, will "remember the fireflies," as Grove told his dearest Kimber in one of these letter poems.

Enjoy *Connections: letter poems to family and friends around the world* by Richard M. Grove (Tai), the son, the father, the grandfather, the husband, the friend – the letterpoet.

Prof. Miguel Ángel Olivé Iglesias. MSc
Poet, Lit Reviewer, Editor, Translator
V.P. of the Canada Caribbean Literary Alliance
Guest Member of the Mexican Association of Language
and Literature Professors

About the Author

Richard Marvin Tiberius Grove, otherwise known to friends as Tai, lives in Presqu'ile Provincial Park where he is publisher of Wet Ink Books and is the Poet Laureate of Brighton, Ontario. He is a Poet, Prose Writer, Editor, Publisher, Photographer, Painter and President of the Canadian Caribbean Literary Alliance. His many titles of poetry, novels, YA novels and memoir can be found at eStores around the world.

He is a graduate of the Ontario College of Art, and Arts Administration at Humber College. He studied art history, religious ethics and philosophy at the University of Toronto, as well as publishing and design at George Brown College.

Kim and Tai
at Bill and Julie's cottage in Presqu'ile

Other Recent Aeolus House Books

Slender Certainties by Mary Lou Soutar-Hynes
The Second Law of Quantum Complexity by Michael Mirolla
Four-Square Poems by James Deahl
Life, after life – from epitaph to epilogue by A. Garnett Weiss
Scar Atlas by Colin Morton
COVID-19 Blues by Barbara Landry
Stronger in Broken Places by John B. Lee
Motion Over Time by Elaine Batcher
A Balance Between Sorrows by Dorothy Sandler-Glick
In the Spaces Between Bonsai by Terry Ann Carter
Homeless City by Donna Langevin and Kate Rogers
Holding Close by Carolyn Taylor
DiVERSity by Margaret Code
The Black Ship by David Clink
Another Open Door by Ann Elizabeth Carson
So That We Might Finger the Words by Sue Chenette
Consider by Susan McCaslin
Everchild by Gwynn Scheltema
Rain on My Skin by Rosemary Clewes
Learning To Leave by Ariane Blackman
To Grace Bridges by Thomas Gannon Hamilton
Digging by Kate Marshall Flaherty
The Fragmentarium and Other Poems by Chris Pannell
Wet Toes by Mary Nyquist
Loose Ends by Ann Elizabeth Carson
The Many Faces by Felicity Sidnell Reid
Towards the Pebbled Shore by Peter Jailall
Travels with Athóma by Daniel G Scott
Timed Radiance by Donna Langevin
Love and Lunch by Mori McCrae
Looking into the Fish Tank by Kent Bowman
The Frailty of Living Things by Carole Giangrande
Becoming History: A Life Told Through Poetry by Blaine Marchand
Bricolage: A Gathering of Centos by A. Garnett Weiss
The Mezzo Soprano Dines Alone by Thomas Gannon Hamilton
Earth's Signature: New & Selected Jackpine Sonnets by James Deahl

www.ingramcontent.com/pod-product-compliance
Lightning Source LLC
Chambersburg PA
CBHW021716120626
46545CB00004B/1584